Marriage

&

Personal Development

Marriage
&
Personal Development

RUBIN BLANCK &
GERTRUDE BLANCK

COLUMBIA UNIVERSITY PRESS

NEW YORK

Rubin Blanck is in private practice in New York. He is a Lecturer at New York University and Adelphi University Schools of Social Work and Administrative Director of the Institute for the Study of Psychotherapy.

Gertrude Blanck is in private practice in New York and is Curriculum Director of the Institute for the Study of Psychotherapy.

Both authors, separately and together, have written articles in the professional journals and, in addition to this book, have co-authored *Ego Psychology: Theory and Practice*.

ISBN 0-231-03150-5

Copyright © 1968 Columbia University Press
Library of Congress Catalog Card Number: 68-9577
Printed in the United States of America
10 9 8 7 6

Contents

Introduction

OUT of the experience in working with marital pairs over a period of many years, I came to an ever-deepening recognition of the extraordinarily complex psychology of the marital relationship. As I examined the more generic nature of specific difficulties which married couples brought for counseling, it became more and more evident that I was dealing with a growth potential which had somehow become arrested or which was distorted or overshadowed by the particular struggle in which the partners were involved. This led me to the consideration of the psychological conditions in marriage in the light of psychoanalytic ego psychology, which conceptual framework provides an opportunity to understand the growth factors in the several stages of the life cycle. I have selected the stage of marriage for intensive study, both its psychology and how counseling procedures can be designed to release the potentials for growth and development within the marital situation.

An ever-increasing segment of the population, finding itself in difficulties which appear to the individuals to be based in their unsatisfactory relationships with spouse and children, is turning to the marriage and family counselor; and a wide range of professional persons is currently engaged in providing counseling in these situations. While marital counseling in some form has been practiced through the ages, and a dearth of advisers in their difficulties was probably experienced only by Adam and Eve, it acquired the characteristics of a distinct discipline in the social agencies within the last two decades.

By no means, however, is marital counseling restricted to social casework. In many parts of the United States, marital counseling is practiced by persons whose formal education is in a related profession, such as medicine, law, the ministry, psychology, psychiatry, psychoanalysis, and others. In fact, practitioners in any of the so-called helping professions may be consulted by the troubled couple and many have developed particular skill in dealing with the problems that such couples bring. The art of working with marital difficulties has also proliferated from the focus on individuals and pairs to families and cultures, and includes sociological and anthropological approaches.

Marital counseling became a major preoccupation in the social agencies immediately after World War II when government took over the responsibility for financial upkeep of destitute families, freeing the private philanthropically supported agencies to devote their attention to family problems which had heretofore been regarded as ancillary to financial assistance. These problems were, of course, marital and parent-child disequilibria, around which social casework had already built up some body of knowledge and skill. Beginning in the 1940s, agencies began to become involved more and more in what they termed *pure counseling*, the attempt to offer help to families on problems arising exclusively from emotional factors rather than those which accompanied financial need. By shifting to this focus, an entirely new field of endeavor was created within social casework, retaining, however, the philosophy of working within the framework of the family unit and at the same time moving into an area which demanded deeper knowledge of human development and behavior, as well as far greater self-awareness and self-discipline on the part of the counselor.

Although certain rather complex skills have always been involved in dealing with family units, even when financial assistance was included, the shift in focus to the more unstructured area of emotional problems necessitated conceptualization to a degree not heretofore thought necessary. Many approaches were and still are being tried. Some of these, such as the attempts to work within time limits and other external factors, have been discarded. Others, such as conjoint interviewing, group treatment of couples, family unit treatment, and the like, are still being tested. Despite the diversity of treatment methods, the consistent factor which is inescapable is that effective counseling calls for the highest level of theoretical knowledge about human behavior and for great technical skill. The exact nature of such knowledge and skill remains at issue, perhaps because marital counseling has not yet become a primary discipline, but derives from other professions, each of which has its unique tradition. Thus, for example, a member of the legal profession might tend in approach to be more authoritarian than the psychoanalyst, whose professional training leads him to encourage self-determination; the physician, because he is often looked upon as wise in all matters, might tend toward offering direct advice more often than the social worker, who is trained to doubt omniscience; the clergyman is expected to offer counseling which is based in religious philosophy. There are also widely varying points of view as to whether marital counseling is at all a profession. The following criteria of professionalization have been established:

1. That there be an intellectual factor and a body of knowledge communicable by education.

2. That there be professional responsibility and high standards of practice, professional organization, and concern with public interests.

3. That education for the profession is prescribed by the profession itself, which maintains control over recruiting as well.

4. That education for the profession must be founded on the general system of education, including integration within the university system.

5. That the profession is licensed and its practitioners enjoy prestige and power.

Obviously, marriage counseling does not meet all these. Nevertheless, several states have begun processes of granting legal status by means of certification or licensing laws, requiring fulfillment of certain prerequisites before a practitioner may call himself a marriage counselor. The American Association of Marriage Counselors maintains that a special training program which would cut across disciplinary lines would provide a sound basis for practice. Psychologists and social workers, on the other hand, believe that their basic professional training equips them for practice. Among the clergy, a relatively recent development is the establishment of an association to set standards for specialization in pastoral counseling. My own view is that with intensive training on the part of the counselor in the understanding of human behavior and in the skillful application of this understanding the distinction between counseling and other forms of psychotherapy tends to diminish.

There still exists some controversy within and among the various helping professions, psychology, psychiatry, psychoanalysis, and social casework, as to whether counselors should be equipped to treat psychopathology in depth. A large segment of the medical profession opposes the practice of psychotherapy by nonphysicians. The discipline of psychology, particularly its clinical branch, regards psychological treatment as its own province and wishes to relegate to social casework an area called "environmental manipulation," which actually has not been the focus of social work since the days of Mary Richmond. Within social work is a spectrum of opinion, there are: those who would eliminate counseling altogether and deal only with intergroup relations; those who would designate as the counselor's province the conscious aspects of behavior only; those who would establish counseling as a distinct discipline apart from psychotherapy; those who believe that, given sufficient knowledge of theory and technique, counseling and psychotherapy coincide. There are also voices within and without the medical profession which dispute the contention that psychotherapy is a branch of medicine. Among these are Freud himself, G. Blanck, Eissler, the Joint Committee on Mental Hygiene, Kubie, and Wolberg.

One of the most challenging technical problems in marital counseling is how to help the person who regards the problem as existing in the spouse, children, job, and other external factors and who cannot see his or her own part in it. Often, therapists dismiss such persons as untreatable. Within the setting of the social agency, where it is traditional procedure to consult with the agency psychiatrist about difficult cases, such consultations frequently result in recommendations for individual psychotherapy, whereupon a referral is made to a therapist outside the agency. Often such referrals are of no avail because the patient continues to regard the problem as external and therefore the therapists find themselves trying to treat persons who are not really ready to be patients in their own right. The person who is possessed of sufficient self-awareness to recognize these problems as stemming from within is likely to seek psychotherapy directly. Those who seek marital counseling are not yet at that point, but tend to regard their problems in terms of the partner or of marital interaction. Social casework has made a major contribution to the difficult technique of enabling the person who thinks these problems are environmental to begin to introspect for the causes of the difficulties. The time-honored concept of beginning where the client is, is casework's counterpart of the psychoanalytic rule that resistance must be dealt with before content. While many therapists are not willing or able to treat a person who cannot acknowledge that he or she has an internal problem, the family counselor in the social agency has developed considerable skill in beginning with the problem as the client sees it and then proceeding to work, via the transference, toward providing insight into the more fundamental internalized difficulties. It is at the point where the shift in focus from external to internal occurs that the distinction between counseling and psychotherapy disappears.

Marital counseling may now be defined as a particular therapeutic procedure designed for individuals who consciously regard their difficulties as stemming from the marital situation. Counseling does not necessarily have as its goal the cure of the internal problems of the individual in the partnership, although that is to be striven for when it is possible of achievement. A more attainable objective in many instances is that of removal of the marital relationship from the arena of struggle. Where the marriage can be freed of the burden of involvement in the two partners' intrapsychic problems, a more benign, growth-promoting medium is provided for each. Sometimes this suffices to undo the impediments to further development; sometimes one partner or both proceeds with individual psychotherapy or psychoanalysis when this further help in the developmental thrust is needed.

Experience and economy dictate that the most useful philosophical and practical approach to counseling is the combination of the enabling and the psychotherapeutic role in the same counselor. Thus the person who comes originally for treatment of a marital problem can be carried through the initial displacement and projection to the phase of acknowledgment of problem within oneself and acceptance of a psychoanalytically oriented treatment procedure. The most obvious advantage of such an approach is that the transference is not disrupted. Some of the more subtle advantages include the application of highly developed theoretical, diagnostic, and therapeutic skills from the very beginning. The importance of the counselor's role in the early phases of treatment cannot be overestimated; it sets the stage for the entire therapeutic process and ultimate success often hinges upon the degree of skill which is brought to bear in the beginning. Counselors, of course, must possess the knowledge which enables them to work in such depth. The marital difficulties are usually presented on a superficial, descriptive level, and, like the proverbial iceberg, the one-ninth that is visible may be the least of the matter. While the remainder that is out of sight to the client may remain out of sight, it is of crucial importance that counselors have a theoretical background that enables them to understand it. The way in which marital partners employ sex, aggression, relationships to children, parents, in-laws, and the like, frequently fulfill unconscious purposes. Instead of the simple technique of mirroring what spouses do to and with each other, the marital counselor is confronted with the need to understand developmental psychoanalytic psychology and to employ concepts such as symbiosis, separation-individuation, ego autonomy, defense, object relations, psychosexual maturation—frames of reference not hitherto thought of as being within the competence of the marriage counselor.

This study of marital counseling pursues a particular theoretical direction, one that I have found to be the most useful in understanding both normal and pathological developmental processes and in providing diagnostic and technical precision. The extension of psychoanalytic theory into the area now known as ego psychology has enriched our knowledge about human behavior and particularly about the way in which the ego develops from birth through the early years of life when the personality is formed. Ego psychology has particular pertinence to the consideration of marriage as a developmental phase because through its generic theoretical propositions regarding growth and development I was able to understand the developmental factor in marriage.

RUBIN BLANCK

Marriage

&

Personal Development

The Traveller

How small of all that human hearts endure,
That part which laws or kings can cause or cure!
Still to ourselves in every place consigned,
Our own felicity we make or find.

Oliver Goldsmith
(Samuel Johnson)

Marriage

&

Personal Development

The Traveller

How small of all that human hearts endure,
That part which laws or kings can cause or cure!
Still to ourselves in every place consigned,
Our own felicity we make or find.

Oliver Goldsmith
(Samuel Johnson)

CHAPTER I

Marriage as a
Developmental Phase

THE designation of marriage as a developmental phase contains the assumption that psychological development continues into adult life and is not, as has been traditionally assumed, confined to the childhood years. While we are more accustomed to thinking of childhood as a preparation for life and, therefore, of adulthood as the life we have prepared for, we are also aware that development goes on during the entire life span. It is undoubtedly correct, of course, to emphasize childhood as the prime developmental period—the time of life when the most accelerated development should take place —and to consider that the experiences and events of this time of life determine the patterning of later modes of behavior. Therefore, the fact that the early years of life are crucial for personality development is in no way challenged here. In fact, it is held that so very much of the patterning of the personality is established in the early years that these will always be the points of reference for diagnosis and for the understanding of behavior, both normal and pathological. In the study of pathology, problems can be correlated with arrests and defects in early development; such reference points then become the focus of treatment. These well-known psychoanalytic facts do not, however, rule out the conclusions from observation of adult behavior that development proceeds throughout life, albeit at a slower pace than during childhood, and that, indeed, failure to develop through the phases of adulthood leads to consequences of arrest and fixation similar to those which are already so familiar with regard to childhood development. This is by no means a new theme, having been elucidated by Erikson in his description of the life cycle, in which he describes the conflicts of age periods throughout life; by Benedek's description of parenthood as a developmental phase; by the several studies of adolescence as a phase in the growth process.

This study of marriage deals with the behavior of people involved in the normal pursuit of happiness. While the situations to be described in later chapters range the entire diagnostic spectrum, from normal behavior to psychosis, and will demonstrate psychopathology in abundance, this remains a study of normal development or, at least, of the attempt of the individuals involved to adapt to marriage and to achieve an ongoing relationship.

When two persons marry, their level of psychological readiness for this step is of crucial importance to the success of the marriage. The most fortunate group of individuals involved may have reached a peak of growth which inevitably impels them into this phase of the life cycle and so enter marriage psychologically equipped to cope with the tasks ahead; a second group may be burdened by the pressures of unresolved or partially resolved aspects of development which will generate difficulties in marriage. For them, success depends upon whether the personality structure of one or both spouses is such that a thrust forward in the growth process can carry along with it some not too pathological deficiencies from an earlier phase. Such good prognostic potential derives its impetus from the natural tendency of a human being toward growth and the progression through the life cycle. In a third group of persons, less favorably endowed, the blocked or incomplete developmental tasks which should have been completed earlier may impede further growth in marriage or may result in the attempt to find in marriage gratifications for which marriage is not designed. Then, frustration of inappropriate desires and the inability to cope with the ensuing disappointment is likely to produce aggression and to result in excessive quarreling, which is the most frequent symptom of disturbed marriages. These latter are the cases to which skilled counseling must be brought to bear because success depends upon whether such persons can be enabled to proceed in their blocked development.

Marriage, then, signals for the first group entry into and for the second and third groups potential for development in at least five major areas of personality growth.

One of the most obvious features of marriage is *the establishment of sexual relations* as an ongoing aspect of the relationship with one specific person. This includes the opportunity for the final working-through of prohibitions and inhibitions of childhood. The prohibitions involve, of course, the incest taboo which, if not burdened with too much anxiety, can now be overcome via sexual relations with a contemporary. The factor of continuity in the relationship is emphasized here because the process is one of gradual attenuation of a taboo within the framework of a relationship broader than sex alone. These inhibitions are present because of the uniquely human condition whereby sexuality exists but cannot be fully exercised in childhood. The lower animals achieve biological maturity and sexuality simultaneously; the human possesses sexuality in infancy and early childhood but must wait many years for biological maturation to make consummation possible. Therefore, inhibition of sexuality in childhood may be regarded as an adaptation to the time lag of biology. Such inhibition is not immediately cast off upon reaching puberty or even adulthood, but may be gradually diminished within the marital relationship.

A second aspect of developmental opportunity in marriage,

complementary to the first, is *the establishment of a new level of object relations.* The concept of object relations (elaborated in Chapter VI) involves the ability to deal with another person on a reciprocal basis and assumes that development has proceeded beyond the desire for gratification of one's own needs only. The normal post-adolescent young adult has long since passed this early infantile level of object relations and is able to regard the other person as having needs, too. When he undertakes marriage, however, he becomes more directly responsible for the relative independence of his own needs and for consideration of the needs of another than at any previous time in his life. How this opportunity is utilized is a factor in further development. Insofar as the sexual relationship is concerned, the level of object relations which has been attained has its effect upon whether sex is employed for self-gratification or in growing appreciation for the mutuality of the act. The phase-specific or time-appropriate development of relatedness to another is best fostered within the continuity of a relationship with one person. This is a different point of reference from that of the strictly moral. Monogamy is here regarded as desirable because promiscuity does not offer the same developmental opportunity.

A third potential for development within marriage involves *the completion of yet another cycle of psychological separation* from the parents. While long before marriage, separation is gradually achieved out of increasing numbers of individual experiences which do not involve the parents, the capacity to choose a partner on a peer level includes readiness to proceed toward further separation. Although complete separation is probably never attained in the human life cycle, developmental processes, nevertheless, lead the individual in that direction. In this sense, marriage constitutes an experience which reaffirms and strengthens this direction by involving the individuals in a permanent relationship with a new person who is not a member of the primary family.

Marriage also provides *increased opportunity for the exercise of autonomy.* Although such opportunity would appear to be a natural concomitant of separation, it is here discussed as another part of the developmental armamentarium because, in marriage, the exercise of autonomy is also an integrative experience. It encompasses the task of maintenance of identity within the paradoxical situation of closeness to another person. The closeness is reminiscent of the infantile dependency upon mother, and yet must not repeat and duplicate this primary relationship. By means of the ego's control * and ability to distinguish between past and present, repetition is avoided. Similarly, maintenance of identity in marriage does not repeat childhood struggle for establishment of identity. The integration of these two simultaneously operating opposites leads to a new level of ego control over both via the integrative process of merging them into a new and no longer paradoxical unity.

Finally, and in part as a result of that integration, *new opportunities for identification are opened up.* In original personality development, stable identifications are established by means of internalization of certain features of the parental personalities. This is not to be confused with the more familiar defensive and pathological process of identification whereby the individual attempts to retain a lost or absent parent by becoming like him or her. In normal identification, part of one's own identity is formed by means of partial identification as part of an ordinary growth process; where there has been traumatic loss, there is less leisure and less selectivity. On the adult level, identification processes carry a quality somewhat different from that in childhood because they occur

* Not synonymous with conscious control.

within a more autonomous climate. There is neither the pressure to retain lost objects nor even pressure to grow because growth is decelerated; therefore, the adult process contains less anxiety and for that reason might even convey a quality of volition to the extent that volition can be thought of as applicable to an unconscious process. It has often been observed that couples who have lived together for a long time tend to resemble each other. This is a manifestation that identification has continued in adult life.

It is now appropriate to define what is meant by a developmental phase. We take as a prototypical model Spitz's concept of the organizers of the psyche (described more fully in Chapter II), in which he holds that a specific achievement of ego development heralds the establishment of a new plateau or level containing the integration of past accomplishments and evolving into a new and higher pattern of functioning. As early as three months of age, the first indication of ego organization appears in the form of a smiling response, signaling the fact that the infant has become capable of a voluntary response to the gestalt of a human face. This is a developmental phase because it contains features which are generic to all developmental phases:

The feature of phase-specificity. This refers to the time factor and means that the event must occur at the psychological moment when the ego is at the point of optimal preparation for its emergence by virtue of having employed past experience to organize the basis for the new level.

The feature of integration. This refers to the ego's function of joining elements from the previous and the new levels and uniting them into a whole greater than the sum of its parts.

The feature of continuity. Each developmental phase constitutes a link in a chain. The potentiality for the transition to the next phase is already contained within the phase which has been reached.

The breadth and scope of the concept of developmental phase can best be understood if it is regarded as one in a series of phases which continue throughout life, from the first organizer to the acceptance of old age. Since we are concerned here with a specific period of life, early adulthood, when marriage customarily takes place, this portion of the life cycle may be examined in the light of the three criteria above. In so doing, the differences between the developmental phases of adulthood and of childhood will also become highlighted. For example, in at least one important feature, marriage differs from Spitz's concept of an organizer. He regards the organizer as an indicator that a new level of development has already been attained. This is not true for marriage; while marriage offers great potential for growth, it is not in and of itself the *indicator* that the ego has achieved a new level. Examining the three criteria in relation to marriage, we find the following:

Phase-specificity. The time factor concerns readiness for marriage. This includes, as stated before, the completion of former phases of development and entails the convergence of psychological readiness with biological maturity.° While biological adequacy is already in existence upon completion of puberty, that state of readiness refers to mating and not to marriage. Marriage requires that the biological ability to mate coincide with the ego's optimal completion of the psychological tasks of adolescence. In this sense, the developmental phase of marriage resembles the phases of early childhood when, similarly, maximum potential is realized as biological

° The distinction made throughout this study between maturation and development is designed to provide accuracy in designating the process as fundamentally biological or psychological. Maturation refers to biologically determined growth and development to the process of growth in which environment and maturation interact. See Hartmann, Kris, and Loewenstein, "Comments on the Formation of Psychic Structure."

and psychological growth proceed in parallel up to a point and then converge.

Integration. Marriage provides the opportunity to integrate all the developmental phases of early childhood, adolescence, and young adulthood. As is true of human development as defined by Hartmann, Kris, and Loewenstein, marriage proceeds within the context of a relationship with another person and affirms this feature of the human condition by the deliberate choice of a partner. Integration is carried out by an ego which has exercised and thereby perfected this function in earlier phases. Now with a new object, consciously chosen for purposes of adult gratification, integration proceeds by following the pattern of former relatedness to earlier objects and yet forming a new, unique relationship, possessed of qualities which no longer resemble those of childhood relationships.

Continuity. The criterion of continuity refers to the place of marriage in the life cycle, constituting as it does the link between adolescence and parenthood. This does not mean that when parenthood is reached, the developmental direction of marriage loses its impetus. In fact, with the onset of parenthood, marriage is obliged to function on an even higher level of integration in order to encompass the new event. It does mean, however, that development in marriage must reach a certain optimal peak before the next phase may be safely undertaken.

To sum up, a developmental phase is one which encompasses a specific period of time; is identifiably different from preceding phases in both time and texture; uses preceding levels of development, transforming them into a new mode of functioning; opens up opportunities for further growth on a newly integrated level; and constitutes a transitional phase in the sense that it occurs in sequence and in relation to the phases which appropriately precede and follow it.

CHAPTER II

The Contribution of Ego Psychology

Psychoanalytically oriented marital counseling has had at its command for many years the concepts of psychosexual maturation, conflict, anxiety, and defense, these having been borrowed from psychoanalytic instinct theory as the theoretical base for the diagnosis and treatment of the individual in the marital partnership. Since the usefulness of this theoretical framework is by now well proved, the dimension added by the formulations of ego psychology provides precision and clarity to both diagnosis and treatment to a degree not possible in working with the older theory only.

The progression of psychosexual maturation may be regarded as the developmental psychology of instinct theory. It enables us to trace individual growth through the familiar and well-known biologically based phases, beginning with the oral and proceeding to the anal and phallic, and to ascribe to each of these characteristic personality traits which adhere to the individual whose maturation remains rooted or fixated in one of these phases. Thus, for example, the oral character is greedy; the anal character is stubborn and parsimonious; the phallic character is exhibitionistic and competitive. Directly pertinent to marital counseling is the concept of genitality, which, in instinct theory, has been described as the final stage of psychosexual maturation. The personality of the genital character is thought to be loving, tolerant, considerate, as well as capable of heterosexual consummation. In a certain sense then, this is instinct theory's description of the marriageable person.

Accordingly, an attempt to account for character traits and their concomitant interpersonal effects in terms of fixation in psychosexual phases requires that theory leap from the biological orientation of bodily zones to the psychological orientation of attitudes toward self and others, and leaves a rather wide gap. While instinct theory provides a very clear explanation of how the erogenous zones become the focal points of instinctual impulses, the development of relatedness between self and others is not adequately explained in terms of erogenous zones and character traits alone. This gap has been filled by ego psychological findings which describe the stages whereby the infant develops from a narcissistic psychic entity, contained within the confines of the mother-child dyad,* to a separated, individuated person capable of loving another. The story of this development is told by ego psychology's description of the growth of personality through the various stages of object relations, beginning with primary narcissism, through need-gratification, and culminating in object love. These stages of object relations and the development of the ego itself proceed in parallel with psychosexual maturation; understanding of how these various facets of personality growth proceed and interact rounds out the understanding of aspects of development which instinct theory alone does not explain.

The concept of the ego existed in psychoanalytic theory from the beginning, but has undergone various changes so that our understanding of it today is different from that in 1900. At that time, it was regarded rather simply as a conscious agent which operated as a counterforce against the unconscious wish-fulfilling agent as, for example, in dreams, where it exercised censorship against the dream wish. By the 1920s, this concept of ego took on more sophistication when it

* Mahler terms this the *symbiotic membrane.*

was recognized that parts of the ego, too, are unconscious and that the ego is a coherent organization of mental processes with a variety of functions—one part of a tripartite system, id, ego, and superego. This recognition, known as the structural theory, fostered an accelerated investigation into the psychology of the ego. First, its role in relation to anxiety was re-examined, forcing a revision of the theory of anxiety per se; shortly afterward, its defensive function was elaborated in detail and the various mechanisms of defense at the ego's command were enumerated and described; following that, consideration was given to its adaptive functioning, and at that point an attempt was made to expand psychoanalysis into a general psychology instead of a psychopathology only. This was made possible by Hartmann's introduction of concepts such as a conflict-free or autonomous sphere within the ego, and of consideration of the ego's adaptive function, lending impetus to investigation of normal development. Perhaps the most important single contribution of those theoreticians who have expanded our knowledge about the ego is the emphasis upon the central importance of the role of the mother upon the development of the infant. The basis for this emphasis was provided by the introduction of the concept "average expectable environment" into which the infant is born, suggesting the arrival of a normal infant into a normal environment and stimulating accelerated investigation into the psychology of normal development. Consideration of how the normal infant's ego develops from part of an undifferentiated matrix at birth to an organ capable of performing a variety of complex and uniquely human functions in the months immediately after birth has occupied the attention of a number of investigators who have contributed complementary conclusions from exploration of this process via several experimental methods, including direct infant observation.

Jacobson elaborates upon some of Hartmann's theories, describing in more detail how the ego, the superego, and the two kinds of drive develop after birth. She pays particular attention to the distribution of psychic energy and shows how the personality structures itself by the employment of this energy as its motive force. At first there is simply an unstructured or amorphous mass of energy and potential. After birth, under the stimulation of the mothering experience, complex development begins to take place. The drives separate into aggressive and libidinal. Some of the drive energy then becomes neutralized, in which state it is no longer available to the drives, but usable by the ego for the further development of its functions. The conflict-free sphere of the ego, containing the inborn ego apparatuses such as perception and motility, also has energy. Thus, the ego, with some initial energy of its own, and additional neutralized drive energy, begins to build up self representations and object representations and to structure the personality. Establishment of self representations and object representations result from continuous daily contact with the mothering person and reflect countless pleasurable and frustrating experiences in the infant's daily life. As these experiences become invested with energy the infant thus endows them with a lasting quality. Gradually, over the first years of life, the self representations and object representations become more stable and more clearly differentiated, making two vital developments possible: 1) the basis for individual identity and for relationship with another person is provided and 2) stability of object representations enables the infant to establish the essential identifications upon which the experiences of identity are founded.

Spitz and Mahler arrive at their conclusions via direct infant observation. Both devote particular attention to the study of the first months of life—Spitz to the first eighteen months, in particular, Mahler continuing her studies up to the third year. Spitz postulates three stages of ego formation which are marked by three "indicators" that such development is taking place. Each of these is directly observable because, at each stage, there is an affective response which indicates that the optimal level of ego organization has been attained.

All theoreticians agree that the first three months of life constitute a definable period of ego growth.* Simple tension-reduction response gives way to a capacity to delay if development takes place within a rhythm of frustration and gratification which, via memory traces, makes gratification predictable and thereby enables the infant to wait for it. Hartmann's particular contribution to the understanding of this period of life includes the postulate that there are inborn ego apparatuses which develop if the environment is favorable; Jacobson's concern with the distribution of drive energy led her to describe the differentiation of the two instinctual drives from an originally undifferentiated matrix; Spitz adds that, by the age of three months, a level of organization of the ego is reached and is signaled by the smiling response. The infant becomes capable of recognizing and responding to the configuration of the human face, which capacity Spitz describes as the first sign of conscious reciprocal communication. Hartmann complements this conclusion with his description of the ego functions and their development, in this instance, the development of the function of intentionality.

Returning to Spitz's scheme, the second indicator is observed at eight months of age when the infant has become able to distinguish familiar persons from strangers. It marks a new stage in the development of object relations in that stability is established and the infant no longer smiles at everyone indiscriminately. Spitz thinks that, at this point, the two drives also fuse, aggression becoming subsumed under libido,

---

* Freud and Hartmann term this the stage of *primary narcissism;* Mahler refers to it as the *autistic phase;* some use the term *undifferentiated phase;* Spitz prefers to call it the *nondifferentiated phase.*

thus providing the basis for the ability to relate to a libidinous object. Also, thought processes begin as the result of the development of a functioning ego.

The third indicator of ego organization becomes evident at approximately eighteen months and is marked by the acquisition of speech. The ability to verbalize the word "no" as a consequence of identification with the aggressor is the indicator of the advent of this stage of development. By this is meant that the infant, having heard the word "no" said to him repeatedly and having experienced the prohibition as an aggression against him, identifies with or becomes like the person who has said "no" to him and is able to say "no" also. From this point, object relations continue to develop at a rate accelerated by the employment of language as the uniquely human means of communication.

Thus, the first organizer structures perception and establishes the beginnings of ego, the second organizer integrates object relations and establishes the ego as an organized psychic structure, and the third organizer paves the way for object relations via semantic communication.

Fundamental to Spitz's theories is the predication that adequate establishment of the second organizer depends upon normal establishment of the first and, similarly, adequate establishment of the second makes the third possible. There are critical periods in the life of the infant when an aspect of psychological development must meet with favorable maturational conditions. Such synchronicity of maturation and development is essential for normal growth. When there is developmental imbalance, the pattern of the next organizer becomes disturbed.

Mahler observed both normal and psychotic children, out of which she proposes a theoretical scheme which describes three phases of development: the autistic phase, the symbiotic phase, and the separation-individuation phase. The autistic phase encompasses approximately the first three months of life, and Mahler's conclusions regarding this phase corroborate the findings of other investigators who have studied the same segment of the life span. All three phases are regarded as normal for development and as points of fixation or regression in pathology. Psychosis is the result of the coincidence of a constitutional ego defect and an environment (mother) that is not sufficiently need-satisfying at the age-appropriate time. Here we encounter the concepts of phase-specificity and rhythmicity in the mother-child dyad. Since the needs of the infant change rapidly with maturation and development, the maternal part of the dyad must be more rather than less attuned to the varying needs of the child. Winnicott has coined the phrase "good enough mother" to describe the adequate but not perfect mother who is flexible and responsive to the child's changing needs, thus providing more gratification than frustration at each point. Mahler, in observing normal mother-child relationships, has found that optimal attunement is not always possible because of temperamental variation, but that normal development can proceed if the arrhythmicity is not too extreme at too many phases. If mother and child are grossly incompatible, however, pathology results. Absence of sufficient gratification in the symbiotic phase, for example, can cause regression to autism; other gross disturbance in the symbiotic phase can prevent development to and mastery of the separation-individuation crisis. Separation-individuation, described as the gradual process whereby the toddler begins to separate from mother both physically and psychologically and to become an individual in his own right, is regarded as psychological birth and takes place approximately three years after physical birth. At all phases, libidinal availability of the mother is essential for the optimal development of ego functions. Her availability serves to coordinate maturation and development so that both more or less coincide. In this way the ego is protected against the failure which may be caused by confrontation with maturational levels for which development of its functions is not adequately prepared. The maturational event of walking, for example, is best mastered when the toddler knows that he can return to mother for "refueling." On the mother's side of this event must be the attunement to his needs, which eventually enables the child to walk away for longer and longer periods of time. When this has been mastered and stable self representations and object representations are built up, the child will be able to tolerate several hours of schooling away from mother. The stage of object constancy is reached: internalization has succeeded and the actual physical presence of the mother is not continuously necessary.

The emphasis upon coordination, timing, phase-specificity, synchronicity, attunement, recognizes that development involves two persons who interact and also that it proceeds best when it proceeds more or less in unison with maturation. Another important factor is that a given developmental phase follow in order of optimum completion of the preceding phase which forms its base. Spitz describes how the inadequate establishment of one organizer burdens the ability to establish the next one satisfactorily; Mahler discusses, in complementary fashion, the effect of incomplete or uneven development; to these, Greenacre adds a new understanding of the nature of trauma. She considers trauma to be more than the event itself because it entails also the coinciding factor of the degree to which the ego is prepared to meet the event at a given moment in development. This adds precision to some well-known observations that an older child, with a more fully developed ego, is better able to master trauma than an infant whose ego is less adequate to the circumstance. Greenacre's concept also allows for the possibility that psychosexual maturation, proceeding as it does according to a biological time table, may in itself become traumatic if it too far outdistances ego development.

This elucidation via the historical origins of ego psychology has reference to the development of object relations, the *sine qua non* of the marital relationship. It demonstrates that this ego function is rooted in the framework of a dyadic relationship, in which optimal growth takes place under conditions whereby maturational and developmental processes are synchronized in an environment which includes the libidinal availability of another person. In an analogous way, marriage also provides an average expectable environment in which a love relationship offers potential for continued growth of the partners and for the creation and growth of new participants in the family relationship.

CHAPTER III

Marriage as a Developmental Phase: Normal and Pathological Sequence

In terms of the ego's readiness, marriage can be undertaken prematurely, belatedly, or for purposes (usually unconscious) for which it was not designed. Elaboration of the almost infinite possibilities for marital difficulties arising from its employment for purposes other than development is the subject matter of the chapters to follow. The over-all nature of these difficulties is touched upon here.

The institution of marriage in the physical, socioeconomic, and legal senses is not in and of itself a developmental phase. The developmental element in marriage is a factor of its psychological aspect. Most marriages in Western culture, where the element of conscious choice looms large, are nevertheless entered into under the influence of strong unconscious determinants. This does not imply that such determinants are necessarily negative or undesirable; they simply exist, and, because they are there, it is impossible to understand this very complex human relationship without taking the unconscious seriously into account.

There are, fortunately, marriages which counselors call "healthy" because, motivated by unconscious forces as is all human behavior, these forces are in the direction of growth and development. Another way of putting this is that the marriage that has been undertaken meets, at least in an approximate way, the three criteria of timing, integration, and continuity described on pages 7 and 8. Although the partners to such marriage will inevitably encounter difficulties and crises, since these are part of life, they undertake marriage equipped with egos which are more or less equal to the task which lies ahead after they say "I do." Our thesis is that these tasks are developmental and must be performed if the life cycle is to proceed in a progressive direction.

In the course of such development, probably the most important single aspect to be worked out is that of identity. Bearing in mind that the crucial months of infancy and early childhood are spent in a state of symbiosis and that identity is acquired by means of differentiation of self representations and object representations, partial identification, and the harnessing of the aggressive drive in the service of separation, identity may be thought of as dearly won and separation never fully completed. It is repeated and "recompleted" many times during the life cycle, but in the final analysis, a residual dependency upon mother remains throughout life and is a fact of the human condition. The repetition of the separation process is most dramatically apparent during adolescence when the so-called "identity crises" are likely to take on turbulent characteristics. They may be regarded, however, as the individual's continuing struggle to differentiate himself or herself and to affirm and reaffirm identity, while the two drives —libido and aggression—exert pulls in opposite directions, the libidinal forces seeking to unite, the aggressive forces seeking to separate. The "no" stage in early childhood and the rebelliousness of adolescence are manifest results of the separation-serving function of the aggressive drive.

When marriage is undertaken, it is almost always under the

impetus of the libidinal drive—the force that unites. Other ways of stating this are that the libidinal forces dictate that an object be chosen for purposes of drive discharge, or, even more simply, that sexual tension motivates the search for the partner. However this is stated, there is universal agreement that marriage involves union. The wedding ceremony itself symbolizes this aspect of marriage—the two become one. The Bible makes it even more definitive—"For this cause shall a man leave father and mother and shall cleave to his wife and they twain shall be one flesh." What then becomes of the striving for identity which was begun in infancy, more or less completed by the third year, continuously reaffirmed during childhood and adolescence, and now apparently disregarded in the single event of the wedding? This is perhaps the point where the completion of earlier phases of ego development is put to a most severe test because, while love conquers all, it does not and should not conquer individual identity or it would conquer the very feature that makes love possible. When the innate striving to unite achieves momentary gratification only, it can be pleasurable without constituting a threat to individuation. Under such circumstances, union takes place in the service of the ego * and identity is not surrendered except momentarily in the sex act. The absence of threat to identity in such fortunate circumstances is a major factor contributing to further development, for the ego free of the task of guardianship of identity and autonomy has energy for further development. The marital experience may then be employed to reaffirm identity and to move forward into the establishment of new roles in object relations. The roles of hus-

---

* Kris coined the phrase "in the service of the ego" to describe the process whereby regression may take place, usually for pleasurable purposes, under the control of the ego, and therefore reversible when the ego no longer deems the regression appropriate.

band and wife become incorporated into the life pattern and pave the way for the next phase in object relations; husband and wife become father and mother to yet another person.

In its more pathological aspects, marriage is employed defensively under the pressure of anxiety and can involve regression and fixation rather than growth. This is not to say that the individuals in even "healthy" marriages are always free of anxiety, nor indeed is anyone. If, however, ego development has been favorable, the capacity to surmount difficulties is present to a greater degree and the outcome of struggle with both internal stress (anxiety) and external problems is likely to be rewarding. This assumes the capacity to experience anxiety as coming from within rather than caused by the partner or other circumstance; in more precise psychoanalytic language, displacement and projection are not employed as emergency mechanisms of defense. If, however, there is excessive anxiety, whether about separation, about homosexual wishes, about oedipal conflicts which must be defended against, the partner is unconsciously chosen to aid in this process and then is used as a defensive bulwark. It is rarely, if ever, possible that another can successfully serve such purposes indefinitely. The almost inevitable failure brings forth the familiar symptoms of blaming the partner as a "second line" of defense. Regressively employed, marriage can be sought as a way of being taken care of and supported, emotionally as well as financially; as a way of acquiring a home instead of making one; as an opportunity to relive conflict in the hope of mastering it.

Thus, marriage can be undertaken as a panacea for unconscious difficulties and sometimes also in the conscious belief that it will solve problems which appear to be practical in nature. It is to these types of marriage that we turn our continued attention in this study of marital counseling and examine the ways in which problems in marriage manifest themselves and how the counselor can work with the partners in alleviating marital disharmony.

The interplay of conscious and unconscious factors in the act of choosing a partner and entering into marriage may be likened to the concurrence of psychic forces which go into the construction of a dream. The conscious reasons for the choice are analogous to the manifest content of the dream, and the unconscious determinants may be likened to the latent content. Because of the interweaving of conscious and unconscious, past and present, conflict, defense, and hidden wish dream interpretation based upon manifest content only is likely to be shallow and to overlook the most important features of the dream. Similarly, marital counseling which does not take into account unconscious as well as conscious, defense as well as adaptation, regressive wishes as well as progressive ones, and the ability of the ego to employ the state of marriage for further growth and development is oversimplified and likely to be ineffective.

As we understand better both the unconscious determinants in the marital relationship and the growth potential that marriage offers, it becomes clearer why the well-intentioned admonitions of the unskilled adviser, based on manifest information only, may be ineffective or even harmful. In the extreme, mate-matching services have attempted to arrange the "ideal" marriage by means of a questionnaire which elicits conscious facts from the individual who is seeking a mate. These data are then fed into a computer which selects the perfectly matched partner. It is hoped by this means to eliminate trial and error. What is eliminated, however, is consideration of those growth-promoting features within the personality which, in conjunction with progressive unconscious wishes, make of marriage an enriching experience if they are present and warn that marriage is being undertaken at some risk if they are absent.

Advisers, often wise and well-intentioned, do think in developmental terms even though they have not conceptualized their thoughts. Thus, marriage is sometimes advised in the hope that it will constitute a cure for some of the incomplete integration of the preceding phase, adolescence. "It will help him settle down." "It will make a man of him." "He needs the steadying influence of a good woman." There is also the thought that a regular outlet for sexual urges will be stabilizing. To illustrate the fallacious nature of such advice within the context of the concept of developmental phases: one would not suggest that the eight-month-old infant who cries at the sight of a stranger be sent to school so that he can get used to strangers. Spitz has taught us that he cries because he is at a developmental stage when such behavior is phase-specific, or in other words, normal. We do not try to cure the manifestations of one phase by suggesting a premature thrust into the next phase. Similarly, the phase of adolescence is marked by turbulence; in fact, absence of such signs of adolescence would cause concern about whether this phase is being adequately transpassed. Turbulence alone, therefore, is not necessarily a sign of pathology, although there can be pathology in adolescence; for example, there can be delinquency, homosexuality, or even psychosis. However, neither the normal nor the pathological symptoms of adolescence can be cured by premature marriage.

Nonetheless, it is from our point of view of great interest that folk wisdom has grasped some inkling of the developmental potential in marriage. We give it conceptual form and structure by dealing with the interrelated aspects of personality as they are brought to bear upon the marital relationship. Consideration is given to the effects of libidinal and aggressive drives, including psychosexual maturation and the fate of the oedipus complex; to the phases of ego development and object relations, particularly to the effect of the symbiotic phase; to the process of identification; to anxiety and defense; to adaptation; to sexual relations; all within the context of these maturational, developmental features as they effect the marital relationship and how pathology results from deficiencies in these various aspects of personality. The therapeutic procedures for dealing with these problems and for enabling blocked development to proceed are detailed.

CHAPTER IV

Sex and Aggression

THIS chapter is not about sexuality, but about the instinctual drives. While at first thought, the relationship of instinctual drive to marriage would seem obvious, some reflection quickly discloses that this relationship is neither direct nor simple. In fact, some of the common misconceptions about marriage include the idea that the sex drive is the only motivating force in marriage and the sole reason for the relationship. Although sexuality is a most important part of marriage, sex and marriage are not the same—nor is sex the only human drive. Here, we discuss not only sex but also the other source of drive energy, aggression,* and we demonstrate how manifestations of each may be recognized, what needs to be understood about them, and how to proceed with treatment.

Turning first to the sex drive, or libido, its role in marriage is best understood if there is cognizance of the fact that originally libido is not involved in genital sex but passes through several phases of maturation before the stage called genitality is reached. The theory is that different zones of the body are erogenously endowed in infancy and childhood and that the dominance of the genital zone is achieved only after these other zones have had their full "lifespan." The first of these

* This is one of several technical terms in psychoanalysis which coincides with a popular word but does not have the same meaning. The popular connotation of *aggression* usually includes hostility, destructiveness, or in the business world, a driving quality as, "an aggressive salesman." While all may be manifestations of the aggressive drive, this term defined in its technical sense is an instinctual drive with energy used in many ways, not always destructively but also in the service of the individual's development and preservation.

zones, the oral, is so termed because the infant, during approximately the first year of life, is endowed with sensitivity in the mouth and the upper part of the digestive tract. The intensity of oral interest is easily observable. The infant is voracious, greedy, ingests food and inedible articles almost indiscriminately, sucks, kisses, bites, and in other ways gives ample evidence of the presence of both libido and aggression, sometimes expressing both in the same act. The oral phase gradually diminishes in intensity after approximately the first year and the "sexual" or libidinal interest shifts to the lower part of the digestive tract. The child is then at the anal phase of psychosexual maturation. At this phase he acquires conscious control over excretory functions and a great interest in them. He experiments with elimination and withholding, with the product of elimination, and with material which resembles it, such as clay, mud, and the like. On the characterological side, the child may be untidy, stubborn, quarrelsome, provocative, generous—again expressing both love and aggression, sometimes alternately, sometimes simultaneously. When this phase passes its peak, it, too, gradually diminishes, giving way to phallic interests. The phallic phase is not yet the genital phase, but a predecessor of it. At the phallic phase, the erogenous zone is not yet employed for sexual union, but much more for body interest, reassurance of intactness, display, competition and envy, admiration, and the like. Again, the characterological features and the mixture of libido and aggression can be observed.

Transition from one of these phases to the next proceeds according to a biological timetable if interference and impediments are minimal, and is best accomplished when the preceding phase has been sufficiently satisfying and has passed its peak. The more or less orderly progression depends not only upon biology but also upon the mediation of the "good enough mother," who provides sufficient but not excessive gratification of the demands of the given phase. In an atmosphere of too much gratification, there results unconscious reluctance to leave that phase or, in more technical terms, a fixation is established; when there is too much frustration, the peak of gratification is never reached and therefore is forever after sought. This, too, results in fixation. A proper balance of frustration and gratification constitutes part of the motive force that encourages maturation, thus aiding the natural biological processes much as proper nutrition aids physical growth. When there is a fixation, it is sometimes diagnostically important to determine whether it is the result of too much gratification or too much frustration.

There is no line of demarcation between one psychosexual phase and another and, therefore, no "graduation exercise" between phases. It is more precise to say that the dominating aspect of one phase recedes because another zone begins to increase in importance. The process may be likened to a wall being built of rows of brick. When the first row is laid, for a while this is the entire wall, and so that is all there is. When the second row is placed, it becomes the top row, built and based upon the first row, which remains, supports, and continues to contribute to the character of the wall. Whether the basic row is evenly or haphazardly set out forever affects subsequent rows. As the third row is added, it in turn becomes the top row, its quality also partially determined by the qualities of the rows upon which it rests. When the wall is finished, it consists of the top or dominant row, with the influence of the other rows an intrinsic part of the total structure.

Each psychosexual phase involving a given bodily zone in childhood may, depending upon the degree of fixation and regression, bequeath to the individual a set of personality characteristics which are rooted in the particular phase and which may be dominant for a lifetime. These are described here and in Chapter II, where reference is made to those characteristics which reflect continued dominance of pregenital sexuality.

Concomitant with the biological maturation which is involved in sexual growth, the ego and its functions, including object relations, develop. The infant then proceeds toward more and more complex tasks which require that he tame the drives in the service of socialization. During the oral phase, the mother is perceived mainly as the giver; in the anal phase, the child begins to learn to respond to the demand of the mother. This demand is qualitatively different from the demand of the oral phase, which was to wait for the feeding, and requires more than simple postponement on the part of the infant; he is now asked to give something. The imposition of such greater demand is age-appropriate because it is within the capacity of the normally developing ego to meet. Thus the infant grows gradually beyond the uneven arrangement of mother/giver–infant/receiver toward increasing mutuality in object relations; ultimately, such growing mutuality will become the pattern for the achievement of genitality. This explains why the genital phase is more than sex alone, as well as why marriages that are too heavily burdened by pregenital desires and one-sided object relations are likely to be unsatisfying.

An important way station on the road to genitality is, of course, the oedipal stage. The achievement of this level of development involves a change in object for both boy and girl, although in the case of the girl this change is more noticeable because, while the pre-oedipal object for both boy and girl is the mother, for the girl the oedipal object is the father. Both sexes, however, undergo similar internal change in arriving at this new level of object relations; they are no longer passive recipients of maternal ministrations, but become active in the wish to do something for the loved one. This points up the importance of looking into the nature of the relationship in seeking the answers to diagnostic questions. In addition to inquiring about who is loved, it is necessary to ask, how is this love offered, or better still, is it really offered or only sought for oneself?

The final stage of psychosexual maturation is reached via the difficult route of relinquishing these oedipal objects too, thus paving the way for the ultimate choice of a nonincestuous partner of one's own generation. Also included in the arrival at genitality are the diminution of ambivalent feelings toward the parent of the same sex; identification with this parent in gender role; and the acceptance of the parents' sexual relationship and of one's exclusion from it.

Returning now to our analogy about the wall of bricks, we can explain more clearly the true meaning of the term *dominance* of genitality. The person whose highest level of functioning is the genital can still enjoy food, drink, smoking, kissing, and pregenital foreplay; can enjoy possessions, hobbies, such as painting and gardening, which are derived from the anal phase; can enjoy competition, admiration, a good appearance, derived from the phallic phase; all without any of these constituting the dominant and preferred forms of gratification and without sexual perversion being more desirable than heterosexual intercourse.

We have already to some extent considered that the aggressive drive functions simultaneously with the libidinous and has its effect upon maturation. This needs to be emphasized here. While the aggressive drive is the source of destructive behavior, it leads to such result only when something has gone wrong in the developmental years of childhood, when the "taming" processes should have succeeded in checking excessive aggression. There are, as has already been touched upon, also positive uses of aggression, such as separation-individuation; the self-possession involved in the ability to say "no"; exploration and locomotion; the exercise of initiative;

self-protection and other forms of self-interest which are at the same time not damaging to others; the healthy self-assertion which is commonly referred to as aggression.

Because manifestations of the aggressive drive do continue into adulthood and often result in the symptoms of quarreling and even violence that make for marital difficulty, it is particularly important to understand how destructive aspects and residues of the aggressive drive can persist into adulthood. In normal development, the aggressive drive fuses with the libidinous sometime between six and eight months of age and becomes subject thereby to the moderating influence of object love. This comes about as the infant becomes able to perceive that it is the same person who both gratifies and frustrates. Since he cannot exist without mothering, he has to make his peace with the knowledge that both good and bad reside in the same person. To put this in more technical terms, the aggressive drive fuses with the libidinous under the influence of an ever-expanding ego which perceives the mother as a whole person. Here is the beginning of object love.

In addition to fusion, neutralization of both aggressive and libidinous drive energy takes place. This process deprives both drives of some energy, which then becomes available to the ego for its further development. Finally, the drives are also subject to sublimation which diverts their aims to socially constructive goals. Thus we have three processes whereby the drives are tamed: fusion, neutralization, sublimation. The libidinous drive has the opportunity also for physical discharge via orgasm; there is no comparable socially sanctioned form of physical discharge for aggression unless perhaps war. We may hypothesize that this offers some explanation for the additional difficulty we have with the aggressive drive and that, finally, after fusion, neutralization, and sublimation, it has to be controlled by a strong and reasonable ego. An alternative hypothesis is that we do not yet have an adequate theory of the vicissitudes of the drives. We do know on a practical level, however, that when the aggressive drive is not tamed, there are resultant difficulties in day-to-day living.

With this brief recapitulation of instinct theory, let us begin presentation of the couples whose marital problems we will study and help to solve. In this chapter four couples are discussed, showing principally the influence of the instinctual drives upon their behavior; in subsequent chapters, other aspects of their problems and those of other couples are discussed. It has been observed by laymen, literary artists, and even comedians, as well as by those in the professions concerned with marital problems, that the two individuals in a marriage are likely to have difficulties which interrelate and mesh in what appears to be an almost uncanny way. The unconscious of each finds echo and resonance in the partner. It is sometimes said that such phenomena form the basis for a "neurotic" marriage. We do not believe that there can be neurotic marriage, only neurotic individuals who are partners in a marriage. It is to these that we now turn our attention, bearing in mind that the artificial and somewhat arbitrary separation of problems into instinctual, ego, maturational, developmental, or the like, is designed for the purposes of study only. In fact and in practice, no such division exists.

Mr. and Mrs. Alfred are a middle-aged couple with adolescent children and have a long history of marital difficulty, which Mr. Alfred feels is caused by his wife's severe emotional illness. She had been in psychiatric treatment for some time before Mr. Alfred came for marital counseling. His initial request is for help in determining both how sick his wife really is and whether there is any hope that a home can be maintained under the difficult conditions which her problems create.

Although overweight himself, he describes his wife as

obese and also describes the harrowing effect upon the family of her desperate, unsuccessful attempts at dieting. The sexual part of the relationship has long been given up. Earlier in the marriage, Mr. Alfred had had some extramarital affairs, but these no longer interest him. He is intensively involved in an active and demanding business and wishes to maintain this level of functioning and to provide a home for his children. He thinks that this is possible within his marriage if he could get either a bit more gratification or less frustration from it. He asks for specific direction in how to help his wife and how to live with her.

The psychiatrist who is treating the wife confirms that her problems are severe. She has had psychotic episodes, periods of hospitalization, shock treatment. She has never really functioned outside a protected setting. In this instance, as in many, the fact that a woman need not function outside the home once she is married and has a family tends to conceal her inability to function within the home.

Further exploration of the household arrangements discloses that Mrs. Alfred has always required her mother to live with them and that some precarious stability has been achieved in this way. It soon becomes clear that, while Mr. Alfred professes that this arrangement is acceptable to him as a way of maintaining family unity for the sake of the children, it meets an unconscious need in him—namely, his own wish to be mothered. His need and that of his wife are stabilized because Mrs. Alfred's mother mothers them both and their children as well. The counselor must bear in mind, however, that this cannot be as idyllic a solution as it appears, for, among other reasons, a woman who produced a psychotic daughter is not likely to have good mothering ability late in life. One must question, therefore, whether the conscious desire for more gratification in his marriage refers to a wish for his wife to function better or rather to the wish that the mother-in-law be a better mother.

In this case, it is fairly obvious that both partners need someone to feed them because they are fixated in the oral phase of psychosexual maturation. Mr. Alfred has reached higher levels of development, and probably of maturation as well, as indicated by his better functioning. It is also of great significance that he does not want to abandon his children simply because he feels dissatisfied. (This is discussed further in the chapter on *Object Relations.*) At this point, it is employed to point up the way in which a fixation may be distinguished from a regression. Mrs. Alfred is undoubtedly fixated as evidenced by the continued presence of the feeding mother and the absence of higher levels of functioning. However, if her oral phase had been a satisfying one, she would not have become so disturbed. Rather, she probably clings to an unsatisfactory mother-child relationship in the perpetual but impossible hope that it will change for the better. She has never been interested in genital sex and it relieves her that it is no longer required. Mr. Alfred, on the other hand, seems to have had more gratification than she in the oral phase, and he has been able to grow, rather unevenly to be sure, in some respects beyond it. It appears, however, that he encountered difficulty —probably conflict and anxiety—at later stages with which he was unable to cope, regressing therefore to the phase where the greatest gratification lay. The marriage represented to him an unconscious solution for his oral needs in a setting in which he is not required to meet in full measure the psychological requirement of being a husband, but can fall back upon a more familiar and comfortable sibling relationship. The diagnostic importance of distinguishing between fixation and regression now becomes clearer. Fixation implies that there has been no forward movement, whereas when there is regression there has been growth beyond the fixation point; such growth is never totally lost. Therefore, although Mr. Alfred yields to the backward pull toward orality, he is still able to maintain certain levels of functioning beyond that phase, for example, in business and toward his children.

In formulating the treatment plan, one considers the real life situation, which in this case includes the fact that the couple is already middle-aged, and thinks about how much further growth is feasible. It seems desirable in this case to try to help Mr. Alfred maintain his highest level of functioning in whatever areas this exists. Psychotherapy or psychoanalysis, which would deal with the anxiety that caused the regression, thus reestablishing higher stages of psychosexual maturation, does not seem realistic nor does he give any indication that this is what he wants. Therefore, the treatment plan is to help Mr. Alfred understand rather than change his needs. For example, he can be helped to become more tolerant of his wife's alternating greediness about food and guilty attempts at dieting if he understands that he finds comfort in food, too. The counselor would also relieve considerable anxiety and guilt by helping him enjoy his ego achievements, in business and in being as adequate a father as he can. This would take pressure off the marriage by diminishing the frustration that results from the search within the marriage for that which it cannot provide.

These are rather limited goals, but the only realistic ones in view of the depth of regression and the degree of pathology, particularly in Mrs. Alfred. Even in such a case, it is not altogether inconceivable that relieving the pressure would perhaps enable Mr. Alfred to regain a stronger foothold in some larger area of the higher levels from which he has regressed. Regression is often more treatable than is fixation because the pathways toward the higher level have already been established, even though later abandoned. In this particular family, the partner with the more favorable prognosis may be enabled to utilize his capacities to some extent in exploitation of the developmental opportunities in this marriage, limited though they may be.

Mr. and Mrs. Bernard have marital difficulty because there are subtle sado-masochistic attacks upon each other which are consciously experienced as painful. Unlike some couples with similar problems, whose unconscious enjoyment of alternating infliction of pain and endurance of suffering has reached a point of stability (e.g., Martha and George in Albee's *Who's Afraid of Virginia Woolf?*), Mr. and Mrs. Bernard come for counseling because they are aware that their bickering is excessive. Mrs. Bernard describes her characteristic way of functioning under stress: "I was so bothered and so completely at a loss as to what to do that I got down on the kitchen floor and gave it the scrubbing of its life." She is hereby describing regression because of frustration and the inability of the ego to cope with the anxiety aroused by a higher level of functioning; the regression is to an anal level. However, it is also evident that this is a partial and temporary regression and that the ego is still intact; even in the regressed state, the ego does not permit soiling but opposes it by excessive cleanliness. Also evident is the aggression in the act and again the ego's control of that as well; she attacks the floor directly and her husband only indirectly. Her very phraseology makes it clear that this is not her highest level of functioning, but one to which she regresses at times of stress. The interpersonal aspects of her act also become clearer as we examine the interaction with her husband. Since this is a typical and repetitious episode in the marriage, we list some of Mr. Bernard's varying reactions to it:

1. Don't wear yourself out, dear. I worry about your working so hard.

2. Why don't you use a long-handled brush instead of getting down on your knees?

3. But the floor is already clean.

4. Why on earth does this house need so much cleaning that it is always in an uproar?

The responses are graded from the apparently benign first to the overtly aggressive fourth response. In reporting such incidents to the counselor, the husband's preface is usually "I can't stand it when. . . ." The statement "I worry" may in fact reflect concern about his wife or, especially if there is no health problem and therefore no reality for concern, may reflect his own anxiety which is activated by her behavior. This anxiety could refer to feeling ignored because of the symbiotic need to have all her attention; to the fear of his own anal conflicts which her excessive cleanliness stimulates; fear of her aggression or of his own, including unconscious wishes that her health might indeed fail.

The first diagnostic fact to establish in treating the husband would revolve around the question of how much it matters to him. This would inform the counselor about whether he can see it simply as an objective event taking place in another person or whether it sets in motion the anxious reactions described above. The second diagnostic step would then be to ascertain which type of anxiety is aroused. Treatment follows in the form of first directing his attention to his inner processes and then of dealing with them in terms of their significance in his individual psychological make-up.

Closer scrutiny of his reactions reveals that none of the four responses is really benign, because none includes an offer to help, nor even indicates an unthreatened readiness to permit the wife to work out her difficulty in the only way that seems possible for her.

Again, we reserve discussion of the ego factors for a later chapter and consider here that these are two persons, drawn together in marriage because one of the myriad unconscious attractions is that both retain a fixation in the anal level. For this couple, this means development has proceeded more or less favorably in infancy, the oral phase was "good enough," but neutralization of aggression was inadequate and carried into the anal phase, where probably there was excessive frustration by overly clean mothers who tried to hasten them through the stage of soiling. Referring once again to our analogy about the brick wall, the next phases—phallic and genital—were reached with more difficulty and are weaker than would have been the case had the earlier phases offered more solid support. We see in Mrs. Bernard that difficulties in living, which another person might find minor, cause her to beat a hasty retreat to an earlier phase of psychosexual maturation in the hope of overcoming the anxiety aroused by the problems she was unable to think through. It is noteworthy also that she has to resort to action rather than to verbalization of thoughts, indicating that neutralization is inadequate. The meshing of her anal problem with her husband's tempts them, unconsciously, to try to gain sado-masochistic pleasure from attacking each other. Because both have reached higher levels, they are not really satisfied with this more regressed relationship when it occurs, but need help in overcoming it.

Where a clear understanding of psychosexual maturation prevails, it will preclude attempts to give advice on casual levels. If it is understood that the anxiety is intolerable, then advising the wife not to be so clean or the husband not to feel so threatened by her housekeeping would not be undertaken. Instead, if it seems appropriate that these matters become the focus of treatment, they would be dealt with individually, with each spouse in terms of his or her own maturation. Even though there is a common element of anal fixation in both partners, the ability to cope with anxiety and the characteristic defenses employed inevitably varies from person to person.

In this instance, the wife employs regression and reaction formation; the husband utilizes projection to preclude awareness of his own anxiety; both employ considerable amounts of unneutralized aggression defensively and simply because it is there.

To recapitulate the technical considerations: the first step in treatment rests upon adequate diagnosis. With regard to psychosexual problems, the spouses' verbalizations in this case give rather clear indication of the nature of the fixation. The second step is both diagnostic and an opening gambit in therapy. This involves an inquiry to determine the source and extent of the anxiety. One might, for example, ask the wife whether she has to scrub the floor or whether she can find less strenuous and enervating ways of working it out. Her reply would enable the counselor to evaluate the degree of anxiety; if the anxiety is too great, then this woman would respond that there is no alternative possible. Whatever her reply, however, the question itself, by requiring her to think about it, has the important therapeutic function of enlisting the most mature and reasonable part of her ego in consideration of the problem. This in itself tends to reinforce the highest level of growth against the tendency to regress. A third therapeutic step is the fostering of neutralization by means of encouraging her to postpone action. Thus, when she feels ready to cooperate, she might herself volunteer to try not to run for the scrubbing brush at the first seizure of anxiety, but to try to bear it without resorting to action. This, if successful, would permit her to learn to substitute thought for action.

The technical suggestions for treatment of the husband involve more difficult procedures because he is not suffering so much from an actual symptom—excessive cleanliness—and is able to project his anxiety upon the wife. Dirt does not disturb him, is his defense; she is the one who has to clean. The counselor would have to lead him slowly via questions designed to involve his reasonable ego in looking within himself. This is accomplished by nonjudgmental questions such as why it troubles him so much, clarifying that his responses are not as benign as he thinks and, especially, why it arouses so much anger. In this manner he would be led, gradually, to abandon projection and to arrive at some inkling of his own anxiety about the same psychosexual considerations rooted in the anal phase, against which he defends differently. This emphasis upon individual treatment is based in the consideration that marriage is only interactive in its more overt manifestations and that each spouse has a different psychological structure and different defenses which only his own ego can be instrumental in changing.

The Bernards' problem is described here as one of the most typical which are brought for counseling. Although the further course of treatment is not discussed here, it is not meant to imply that treatment ends at this point. An alternative treatment plan for Mrs. Bernard would, for example, include consideration of the desirability of encouraging regression within the context of the transference relationship with the therapist rather than simply fostering functioning beyond the anal level. This form of therapy in depth is designed to undo fixation and permit maturation to proceed to higher levels. It is analogous to removing the upper rows of the brick wall and then repairing the rows that are defective. Granted that this kind of therapy calls for training and skills beyond those of many marriage counselors, it may not be precluded.

For both Mr. and Mrs. Bernard, counseling short of depth therapy might, nevertheless, succeed in promoting development. This is accomplished by means of diminishing the opportunity for gratification of the anal sado-masochistic instinctual desires, by encouraging, as described, each partner to understand and control his and her part in it. As such pregenital enjoyment diminishes, this couple might begin to enjoy more "adult interaction" with less anxiety. If anxiety remains too great, they would at least seek further help with overcoming this impediment to the employment of marriage as a developmental phase.

There are other symptoms and manifestations of anality which are rather frequently encountered in marriage counseling. Foremost among these is quarreling about money. Behavior such as stinginess and its opposite, profligacy; the tendency to collect and its opposite, to disperse; and other inconsistencies which confuse the partner because the anal phase is marked by ambivalence and alternation, all confront the counselor with problems which are based in anality. Also, provocation to sado-masochistic interaction and veiled and overt manifestations of aggression indicate the presence of anally motivated behavior.

A male clerical worker, mild-mannered to the point of timidity, middle-aged and resigned, seems to know exactly how to "help" his wife by cleaning up the kitchen for her. In so doing, he points up what he considers to be her inefficiency and slovenliness by doing over again and presumably better some task which she may have just completed.

A woman who wishes desperately to please her punctilious husband tries clumsily always to be on time and usually thus manages to be late. So common is this kind of veiled aggression that it is the subject matter for humor in movies, television, comic strips, and the like. Those who find Mr. Bernard's second response amusing—"Why don't you use a long-handled broom?"—recognize and respond to the disguise of aggression as solicitude.

The task of dealing with the manifestations of the aggressive drive on the level of individual treatment presents no fewer difficulties than it does on the level of groups, races, and nations. It is always easier to deal with libidinal than with aggressive aspects of behavior. The counselor's own maturity and development are put to a most severe test in his work with the processes of "taming" aggression. A different countertransference problem is involved: since aggressive behavior is designed to hurt and threaten, whether the counselor can remain unthreatened depends very much on how successfully he has mastered his own developmental tasks and has become at least as comfortable with aggressive tendencies as with libidinous.

Frequently encountered rationalizations between marital partners are based on their own experience in interaction. One spouse provokes; the other responds; then they alternate; provocation justifies retaliation. It is a striking fact, often observed by experienced marriage counselors, that whenever the capacity to postpone drive discharge is developed and increases, neutralization renders impulsive action superfluous and the interaction ceases simply because there is no longer any pleasure in it.

Another and perhaps even more important aspect of dealing with aggression concerns the fact that when defensive struggle is most intense, important bastions are being threatened. It has been said earlier that the aggressive drive serves the important function of aiding in the establishment of identity by furthering the process of separation. Where identity is threatened, then aggression must be summoned to maintain it. This concept has direct application in counseling and forces us to reconsider the positive uses of aggression, thus tempering attempts to eliminate it as altogether undesirable. Mr. Bernard, for example, felt more threatened by his wife's floor-scrubbing than his aggressive-facetious remarks reveal. Despite many jokes to the contrary, it is difficult for a man who has worked his eight-hour day to relax and read the newspaper while his wife labors. Compassion and identification, if carried to their logical conclusion, would result in Mr. Bernard's doing more housework than would be comfortable for his masculine identity. If his aggression is understood as, in part at least, defending his masculinity, then the counselor will support the purpose even if he does not necessarily encourage the method.

Mrs. Charles's complaint about her husband is that he does not want children. She is in her early twenties; he is thirty-two. Exploration reveals that whatever his ultimate intentions, at this point he is saying that he is involved in building a career (law) and wants to defer having a family until he becomes better established. This causes Mrs. Charles an inordinate amount of distress, leading to quarreling, from which she emerges in a depressed state. It is because of the depression that she seeks counseling.

She feels that life is not worth living if she is denied immediate fulfillment of her wish for a child. Typical of such cases, the wife's hope is that in some way the counselor will be able to force the husband to give her what she wants. She marshals impeccable logic. There is enough money even though Mr. Charles is finding himself professionally somewhat late; she does not have excessive material demands; he should have children before he is too old to be an active father; she loves children. Truth and justice march in her camp, while he is depicted as simply unreasonable.

Mr. Charles is puzzled because he cannot comprehend the urgent quality of her desire for children. This is his second marriage, and he prefers to have more time to work out the marital adjustment and to be more certain about it than before. He takes into account that his wife is young enough so that waiting a year or two cannot matter much for childbearing purposes. He feels pressured and, accustomed in his profession to logical thinking, becomes baffled and, finally, indignant at Mrs. Charles's apparent illogic. The counselor begins to realize that the adaptive nature of his reliance upon logic, so useful to him professionally, is a defense against feeling, which results in rigidity in emotional situations where logic is of little avail. Here we have the interaction; Mrs. Charles's unconscious needs clash with Mr. Charles's defensive system. Both employ logical arguments in their quarreling, which does not have the desired effect of relieving the anxiety because it does not succeed.

The counselor's explorations have to be carried out with great tact lest the inquiry into the urgency to have a child appears to Mrs. Charles to contain the same quality as Mr. Charles's logically doubting questions and link the counselor's inquiring attitude in her mind with her husband's objecting one. The counselor is aware that her conscious answers must be carefully weighed because she is unaware of her unconscious motive. In such instance, the best safeguard to treatment is the patient waiting for the development of a positive transference which will enable her to offer clues to the unconscious in an atmosphere of trust.

A puzzling diagnostic question arises in this case. Since she married a man somewhat older than herself, unresolved oedipal wishes are suggested. However, such evidence is thin. The counselor looks for substantiation. She had always dated older men, including her employers, and her husband was married to another woman when she met him. Nevertheless, the choice of the level on which to work is dictated by the verbalizations, after the establishment of the transference: "I feel so incomplete. . . . I feel empty inside. . . . I just love the idea of a baby growing in me. . . . My husband has his profession and I have nothing." While the exploration around her preference for older men does not lead to much, pursuit of her feeling that she lacks something brings confirmatory memories of the counselor's hypothesis that she is in the stage

of phallic envy. She is the elder of two daughters. The father
wanted a son and in many ways treated her as such. She had
always been a tomboy, "never afraid to do things."

The wish for a baby now becomes understandable as an
urgent need to equalize the marital relationship in terms of a
childhood residue of phallic competition. In her unconscious,
she suffers from a physical deficiency while her husband has
everything. The anxiety about her fantasied castrated state
becomes unbearable; the baby is needed to alleviate this.
With this understanding, the urgency becomes comprehensi-
ble, for while it does not seem too much to ask that a young
woman postpone motherhood temporarily, it is now another
matter altogether. On Mr. Charles's side, there is a concordant
unconscious note. While so much is demanded of him, he
must maintain his physical intactness against an unconsciously
sensed demand that he provide his wife with a penis-baby.
This strikes him in an area where he, too, has much anxiety.
His successful defense against fears for his own intactness,
namely, functioning professionally with an effective intellect, is
threatened at home. He can do nothing but refuse rigidly to
yield.

The procedure in this case is to help both partners become
aware of the defensive nature of their behavior, largely that
logic is employed and seems so convincing not because it is,
but because it is needed to defend against anxiety. Effective
counseling requires that the counselor not be taken in by the
impeccability of such conscious reasoning. Well-educated persons, accustomed to using their intellects, can and do summon
reasonable sounding arguments to allay anxiety about less rational, unconscious ideas. It is important that the counselor
avoid not only joining the argument or taking sides but also
haste. The trusting, positive transference is essential and only
develops in time. When it does, the individuals in the partnership may be prepared for deeper therapy. It is desirable that

the counselor have the skill to continue with such persons in depth in order to utilize the already established transference. However, when this is not possible, transfer to a psychotherapist or psychoanalyst may be made when the partners understand their defensive systems somewhat and have even had an opportunity to experience some of the underlying anxiety.

Mr. and Mrs. David come for counseling principally because there is so much quarreling about relatively trivial matters. Careful exploration of these incidents by the counselor discloses a rather interesting pattern. It seems that Mrs. David is wont to find reasons to delay and matters to fuss about whenever she senses that her husband may be interested in making sexual overtures. The quarreling is reported to take place two or three times a week and usually results in Mr. David's sleeping on the living room sofa. Probing more deeply into the individual characteristics of each partner and some of their history, the counselor finds that Mrs. David is a childlike person, with certain girlish qualities which make her rather charming, but whose life style seems to be one of playing house rather than taking herself seriously as a married woman. Mr. David was attracted to her evident charm and feels protective toward her. He is seven years older than she, a rather serious-minded person who enjoys being leaned on and who makes all large and small decisions for both of them. It becomes clear to the counselor that in this marriage, Mrs. David is reliving a deep attachment to her father and that conflict arises around the sexual aspects of the marriage because the unconscious equating of husband and father raises the incest barrier.

On Mr. David's side, the counselor learns that he is the eldest son of a widowed mother and shouldered paternal responsibilities toward his younger siblings. It would appear on a superficial and conscious level that such a marriage is tailor-made. Examining it more deeply, however, one finds that the very attractions are also impediments. Mrs. David cannot understand and deal with wishes which are repressed and therefore unknown to her. Mr. David is reliving a role which gave him much comfort in his early years. He not only gained status, authority, and approval for his paternal behavior but, at the same time, compensated for the loss of his father via identification with him. Both partners are distressed and bewildered by the unsatisfactory sexual relationship, but cannot understand the reasons behind it.

It is all too tempting in such a case to treat the sex problem in the narrow sense. If it is diagnosed as sexual frigidity, it is possible to treat that single aspect with apparent success. There are credible reports of mechanical instructions which enable husband and wife to enjoy sexual contact. We use the term *contact* rather than experience or relationship in a considered way. Orgasm can be achieved outside marriage as well as within; in homosexual encounters; or in autoerotic activity. The studies of Kinsey and of Masters and Johnson leave no doubt about this. These are not the same qualitatively, however, as orgasm which constitutes but one of the myriad experiences within the context of a relationship which continues to develop throughout life.

For Mr. and Mrs. David the treatment of choice is one which takes into account that both partners have unconscious oedipal conflicts which will continue to color their relationship to one another and certainly to their children, even if the symptom of frigidity were to be relieved. The question regarding treatment plan is analogous to whether to provide aspirin to relieve a headache or to search for causes. Our approach deals with causes. Therefore, the initial phases of counseling would engage these partners in the desire for a cure which would be more lasting and more gratifying than a symptomatic one. Since they have gone a long way up the developmental ladder, they bring to the treatment situation their favorable life situation, including the capacity to wait and therefore to work things out slowly and thoroughly. The first step, again, is to await the development of trust via transference. If possible, and it usually is, the sometimes subtle manifestations of residual love for the oedipal object may be pointed out in the transference. Ultimately, psychoanalytic treatment would be desirable, with the same counselor if he is able or with a psychoanalyst via transfer. The plan in the beginning should encompass the possible end goal. Therefore, it would be desirable in this, as in most cases, that the two spouses begin with two different counselors. This has the advantage of providing for the least disruption in transference.

There are some cases which masquerade as oedipal and appear so at first glance, but are based in earlier levels of growth. Not every woman who marries an older man is seeking her father; nor is every man who remains devoted to his mother fixated on the oedipal level. It is necessary for the counselor to look in such instances for the possibility that the spouses are involved in the search for someone to take care of them. Separation anxiety—the fear of emergence from symbiosis—can manifest itself as the clinging to another which may be mistaken for oedipal or sexual behavior. If the sexual wishes toward the parent are frank and open, the situation is more ominous diagnostically because it indicates that there has been failure to repress and that the ego is therefore inadequately developed. Such cases ought to be treated more cautiously than the four more usual counseling cases we are describing here. There is, in these instances, less ability to respond to confrontation, inadequate frustration tolerance, diminished capacity to enter into a transference which can be distinguished from a real relationship. Such cases would be diagnosed as closer to borderline categories and the therapeutic goal would be different, involving the long-term process of helping the individual build a less defective ego.

In considering how marriage constitutes a developmental phase insofar as the drives are concerned, the distinction between maturation and development on page 7 once again becomes useful. Since maturation is essentially biological and will proceed unless there is gross interference, then we may say that marriage offers the potential for satisfying the adult manifestations of the drives. It has been observed that, without marriage, there is arrest. This is so because within our social structure, marriage is the medium for sanctioned fulfillment of drive requirements.

In the chapters to follow, more is presented about the many-faceted aspects of diagnosis, including ways of distinguishing among the phases of maturation and development. Here it was intended to stress the diagnostic importance of determination of psychosexual level in the treatment of marital problems, and the influence of drive-motivated behavior upon the marital relationship. To propose to end consideration of the drives at this point may be thought remarkable in that the drive that constitutes the major aspect of marriage has barely been touched upon. However, it has already been indicated that sex is more complex than mere drive discharge. Since our thesis is that marriage is a developmental phase which is based in a relationship—that is, in object relations—the ego functions which play such a large role in the developmental features of a relationship must be given consideration before the place of sex in marriage can be understood within its broader context. Therefore, a discussion of sex, in a later chapter, follows consideration of the ego and its functions.

CHAPTER V

Problems of Symbiosis and Separation-Individuation

THE developing individual's first experience with another person in early childhood patterns his relationships to self and others throughout life. Here, let us look at the more general aspects of the relationship to self and object and how certain types of marital problems can be understood in terms of patterns laid down in childhood.

Mahler and her co-workers have elaborated a developmental scheme, described in Chapter II, which delineates normal and pathological modes of relatedness and thereby extends our understanding of problems that are likely to arise in the marital relationship. She proposes that the newborn infant is, for approximately the first three months of life, in the autistic phase during which there is no awareness of self and other. The gradual awareness that needs are fulfilled from without leads the infant into the next phase, symbiosis, in which the mother, at first dimly perceived, is assumed to be part of the self. As is true of all human development, the experiences in the symbiotic phase must gratify the need of that phase, which is closeness, in order for the need to diminish and for the developing child to move into the next phase which Mahler has termed the separation-individuation phase. Here, again, there is no clear line of demarcation between one phase and the next; late symbiosis blends in with early separation-individuation. It is via the ultimately more gratifying experiences in the separation-individuation phase, after a satisfying symbiotic phase, that the child emerges from the "symbiotic membrane" and gradually acquires identity as an individual separate from the mother. By separation-individuation, Mahler clearly means an intrapsychic, developmental, gradual process of separation of the self from the object and the beginnings of individual identity. She does not mean physical separation. Her scheme allows for consideration of the changing psychological needs of the developing individual and postulates that, for optimal development, the mother be attuned and responsive to these alterations. Thus, the mother must be able to constitute a symbiotic partner for the child when the child is in that phase of development, and must be able to relinquish this role and become, in Mahler's term, the "catalyst" of separation-individuation when development has proceeded to the point where the child is ready for that.

Persons with problems rooted in the autistic phase are not likely to attain marital status, nor even to function at large in the community. Those with problems which have their origins in the symbiotic and separation-individuation phases, abound, however, and present themselves to the marriage counselor. Recognition of the developmental origin of these problems enables the counselor to deal with them with precision.

It must be borne in mind that these developmental phases are normal for early development and only become pathological if fixations in and irreversible regressions to these phases persist in later life. The child in the first year of life who experiences self and mother as one is going through a normal growth process; the spouse who experiences the self as part of the marital partner is in a pathological condition and does not have the separate identity which is the normal consequence of adequate transition from symbiosis through separation-individuation. In diagnostic terms, such phenomena in adults are often characteristic of borderline personalities. Allowance is made, in our consideration of this subject, for regression in the service of the ego because, in the intimacy of the marital relationship, there are moments when there can be a temporary and reversible regression to symbiotic union—at the moment of orgasm, for example.

While the symbiotic phase in childhood is characterized by a feeling of "oneness," the separation-individuation phase is one of back-and-forth movement. The intrapsychic movement is often paralleled by the external, physical activity. The normal toddler, with increasing locomotive, verbal, and manual skills, strikes out on his own, experiences mild doses of separation anxiety, returns to mother for "refueling," ventures forth once again, and so on until identity and object constancy are achieved (see p. 12) and "psychological birth" takes place. It must be iterated that separation-individuation is, in normal development, relatively rather than absolutely completed. A tendency to regress to the symbiotic phase remains throughout life, and one is particularly likely to long for maternal reunion at times of stress.

Some of the marital problems which were presented and discussed in the last chapter in the light of instinctual drive and psychosexual maturation now may be examined from the aspect of the symbiotic and separation-individuation phases in the development of the individuals involved. Fixation in and regression to these phases affect the modes of relatedness.

In the light of what we now know about symbiosis and separation-individuation, it is apparent that Mrs. Alfred remains largely fixated in the symbiotic phase and has not completed the process of separation-individuation. She not only lacks a sense of identity, she has not even been able to attain a degree of physical separation from her mother. Although psychological and physical separation are not the same, and one can be separated and individuated in Mahler's sense even though physically together, in an adult, the inability to tolerate physical distance from the mother usually indicates that psychological separation, too, has not taken place. Mrs. Alfred is able to function as a wife and mother in a minimal way and needs her own mother as an extension of herself in the performance of the marital and maternal roles. It is truly as though, together, they constitute one person.

Why then, since Mrs. Alfred's symbiotic tie to her mother has persisted since infancy, has she married? We have said that psychological prerequisites for marriage include the completion of the developmental tasks of childhood and adolescence, psychological and physical separation from primary objects, independence, and the ability to form a relationship with a heterosexual partner of one's own generation. The facts of Mrs. Alfred's psychological condition do not meet these criteria. Our speculation about her early development included consideration of the absence of optimal oral gratification in infancy, thus accounting for the persistence of preponderantly oral needs in adulthood. Since her mother continues to feed her and, indeed, since she has survived to adulthood, it is not likely that the nutritional aspect of mothering was grossly inadequate in infancy. The symbiotic phase of ego development coincides with the oral (and later with the anal) phase of psychosexual maturation, and it is in this area that her mother had not been able to gratify her sufficiently to enable her to attain optimal satisfaction and to proceed to higher stages of development relatively unencumbered by persisting oral-symbiotic needs. For purposes of theoretical exposition, we have here the opportunity to examine how maturational and developmental processes proceed side by side and why, in this case, oral gratification alone in the narrow sense of nutritional adequacy did not provide opportunity for psychological growth even though the obvious physical growth did take place as a result of the feeding.

We find, by such examination, that Mrs. Alfred's psychological problems arose in the early months of life when her mother was not attuned to her symbiotic needs. Then, at the age when she should have reached the separation-individuation phase following a gratifying symbiotic experience, Mrs. Alfred was already far behind the average child in her psychological development. She typifies certain kinds of psychotic and borderline disturbances which have their roots in a troubled, arrhythmic symbiosis because mother and child are not well attuned. By the time normal separation-individuation processes should have begun, Mrs. Alfred and her mother were not only locked in an impasse of unsatisfactory symbiosis but were presumably unable to enter the separation-individuation phase prepared to carry out the more distinct roles which are phase-specific at that time—the child who experiments with toddling away and returning time and again, the mother who "catalyzes" that process by encouraging the separateness and by making herself available when the child needs to return for "refueling." For Mrs. Alfred, the dramatic evidence of her mother's continued, phase nonspecific involvement in the developmental phase of marriage attests to the probability that there was lack of attunement in earlier phases as well.

The fact that Mrs. Alfred did marry, nevertheless, must be taken into account and may be explained by consideration of the human tendency toward growth. There must have been some forward thrust. Freud likens some of the tenuously held forward positions to the situation of an army which has its main forces in the rear, but maintains some weakly held positions ahead. The marriage, which undoubtedly was undertaken for unfavorable unconscious reasons, such as continued symbiotic wishes, may nevertheless be regarded as an attempt to move ahead developmentally.* It is burdened, however, by too

* In Chapter VIII there is a discussion of the defensive function of the marriage.

much failure of earlier developmental phases. Thus, Mrs. Alfred is unable to deal with her husband as a separated individual. She regards him as part of herself because this is consistent with the symbiotic mode of relating. Here lies the deeper explanation of Mr. Alfred's complaint that there is so little gratification for him in the marriage. Since Mrs. Alfred has little or no conception of him as a separate individual, it follows that she is able to gratify him not in accordance with his needs but only as she perceives them to be.

If this aspect of Mrs. Alfred's problem is understood, then her treatment, whether undertaken by the marriage counselor with sufficient training to go into such depth or by the psychotherapist, psychiatrist or psychoanalyst, will support the weak forward positions and endeavor to help her move the "main forces" beyond the oral-symbiotic fixation to higher levels of development. This would involve enabling her to grapple with the heretofore avoided separation-individuation crisis. While the prognosis is rather doubtful, one would not wish to deny her this therapeutic opportunity or at least the opportunity to test out her growth potential.

We have already speculated that Mr. Alfred has progressed, in his childhood development, to a point somewhat beyond that of Mrs. Alfred. To perfect our understanding of the convergence of intrapsychic problems in the marital interaction, it is necessary here to mention another developmental concept, that of uneven development. We have already shown how Mr. Alfred appears to suffer from regression to and fixation in the oral phase of psychosexual maturation and how this dovetails with Mrs. Alfred's dominant psychosexual phase. It does not follow, however, that ego development necessarily proceeds in parallel with drive maturation. While such even development is most desirable, only the more fortunate and therefore more normal individual is likely to have been able to accomplish such coordination under the auspices of good mothering, for it is the mother whose task it is to guard against one-sided development such as the drives outpacing the ego's ability to cope with them.

In the case of Mr. Alfred, it is assumed that, while regression to the oral phase occurred, the ego did not similarly regress, as evidenced by his adequate functioning in business and in relation to his children. Therefore, while he seeks oral and symbiotic gratification unconsciously, it is not wholly satisfying even when attained because it conflicts with and challenges his identity and masculinity. This disparity is the prime source of his discomfort and constitutes the motivating force in his search for help.

The treatment plan for Mr. Alfred now includes the concepts of symbiosis and separation-individuation and continues to support the higher levels of ego functioning and to enlist his intellect (an ego function) in the service of understanding that which cannot be changed. With regard to symbiosis and separation-individuation per se, one would encourage him in the reinforcement of identity, including masculinity (gender identity). At the same time, there must be tolerance for symbiotic regression, which is best fostered in an atmosphere that neither condemns nor encourages it at the expense of higher levels of relating. Granting that such treatment calls for great skill on the part of the counselor, it must also be granted that the benefits are far greater than those to be derived from dealing with the more conscious aspects of the marital relationship only.

In the case of Mr. and Mrs. Bernard the symbiotic problems are less intense and occur only at moments of stress. Both partners in this marriage have more or less mastered the separation-individuation phase and, insofar as identity problems may at times persist, these may be traced to the latter stages of the separation-individuation phase. (This may be compared with Mrs. Alfred's genetic problem which lies in the earlier phase of symbiosis.) That Mrs. Bernard has a fairly intact ego and sense of identity is evidenced by the functioning of her defenses and by her ability to substitute symbolic rather than direct gratification of primitive wishes. She does not soil, she cleans; she does not strike her husband, she implies by indirection that he is dirtier than she. Her very act of scrubbing the floor is an independent one, although motivated by anxiety that brooks no delay.

Mr. Bernard, who sought counseling because his wife's behavior is so troublesome to him, appears to be functioning better because he has no manifest symptoms. However, his psychological balance is more precarious precisely because he is less able than is Mrs. Bernard to resort to stable defensive behavior. He is unaware that he is threatened by his wife's absorption in housekeeping because it leaves him out; put another way, this means that his unconscious symbiotic wishes are frustrated by her independent act, that is, her need to deal with her anxiety in her own way. If we look beneath his complaints, therefore, we find that he is really saying that he feels left out, abandoned, alone. In Chapter IV, we suggest that the counselor, in treating Mr. Bernard, attempt to ascertain what kind of anxiety distresses him. Here we propose that it may very likely be separation anxiety, the kind of anxiety that ensues when the symbiotic tie is threatened.

This is such a prevalent problem in marriage that numerous examples can be cited from everyday practice of marital counseling. The wife who resents her husband's every moment with others—colleagues, friends, relatives, even their own children—may scold and thus provoke quarrels over matters which are based in her symbiotic wishes. "He comes home from work and reads the paper in the evening" may be simply expressive of the housewife's loneliness and isolation in the course of the day. It may, however, represent resentment based upon the unconscious assumption that he is part of her and may not carry on any independent activity. When such a case presents itself for counseling, the counselor has the delicate task of first ascertaining that the marital dispute is actually founded on symbiotic wishes which are believed to be valid. In terms of the individual's psychic reality, there is indeed validity and he becomes untreatable by a counselor who attempts to gainsay it. One cannot simply declare to the complaining wife that her demands are unreasonable, nor lecture her on her husband's right to read the newspaper or to watch television after a day's work. To her unconscious, he is part of her and therefore it is eminently reasonable that he devote himself wholly to her. The counselor who can diagnose the symbiotic nature of the demands, and who can empathize with their cause, will be able to help the distressed spouse understand them and perhaps ultimately to conquer them. It is not intended to imply here that such understanding is conveyed by directly informing the individual of his symbiotic problem, but rather that the counselor who is equipped to deal with problems on this level can promote considerable growth; the counselor who is not trained in depth psychotherapy will at least be nonjudgmental if he understands the theory of ego psychology.

Similar symbiotic problems may become manifest in the complaint of a husband that, when he arrives home in the evening, his family does not drop everything in order to devote themselves exclusively to his needs. "She is always busy with the children when I come home and hardly notices me." "My dinner is never ready when I come in." "She cares more about getting out to her bridge club every Monday night than about staying home with me." These are some of the variations on the symbiotic theme to which the counselor must be alert. Translated in the counselor's mind, they become, "How can she, who is part of me, function as though she is a separate individual?" "I cannot bear it because it leaves me feeling incomplete." To persons with such thoughts, it is bewildering and incomprehensible to talk with them about the rights of others. In their unconscious, there is neither self nor other, but a union of the two.

Another facet of the same problem, and one which constitutes a rather common cause of marital difficulty, results from the disappointment of the symbiotic wish when the marriage has been undertaken, unconsciously, for purposes of its fulfillment. Such problems are prime examples of how marriage may fail when entered into for purposes for which it is not designed. In part, Mr. Alfred suffers from such disappointment. Mrs. Alfred, locked forever in the symbiotic phase with her own mother, seemed attractive to him in the courtship period precisely because her symbiotic mode of relating held out promise of meeting his own symbiotic needs. Unconscious logic may lead the young man or woman to become involved in marriage because the mate is thought to provide the solution to the longing for continued union with the mother. The symbolism of "the two become one flesh" is taken literally; the developmental phases which follow the symbiotic phase are skipped over and premature marriage takes place. Prematurity refers here not to chronological age, but rather to the fact that the orderly developmental progression is short-circuited. The developmental sequence requires that the young adult enter into marriage having completed the developmental tasks of childhood, particularly separation-individuation, and of adolescence; only then will the next developmental phase —marriage—hold out promise of success. Under such favorable circumstances, another step in the separation-individuation process is carried out; the ties to the primary family are loosened and a contemporary is chosen with whom there can be moments of symbiotic gratification within the larger context of a relationship in which individual identity is well-established.

It often happens that a man who seeks to replicate symbiotic union with a mothering person may seem to have achieved this goal in marriage because, sometimes, the external manifestations of the marital arrangements lend themselves to this deception. If the wife cooks, keeps house, does his laundry, and performs other domestic tasks, it may appear as though he has found another mother. Gradual disappointment, in such instances, often bursts out full-blown when a child is born and the wife enters into symbiotic union with this new person. While such relationship between mother and child is appropriate when it is phase-specific for the child, the husband cannot tolerate being left out. Understanding the intensity of his own symbiotic needs in such circumstances clarifies for the counselor why he is unable to adopt the roles which are appropriate to higher phases of development—husband and father. It is particularly advantageous, in counseling, if the couple should come for help before the developmental phase of parenthood has compounded the problems of incompletion of the developmental phase of marriage. Disappointment in the failure of the marriage to gratify inappropriate symbiotic wishes can be detected by the counselor in such mundane statements as, "My wife does not understand me." The counselor must explore such complaints to ascertain whether the husband has, in fact, verbalized the wishes which the wife has failed to understand for, an important aspect of symbiosis is that the partner can know one's thoughts. Such assumption is based upon the unconscious idea that the other person is part of the self and that one can understand oneself without words. Thus, the wish to be so understood without verbal communication can, in the treatment situation, be used for diagnostic purposes in identifying the existence of a symbiotic wish.

The woman who enters marriage with the unconscious desire for a husband who will be a symbiotic partner is perhaps in greater difficulty. Some men, in identification with their own mothers, have feminine traits. Such identifications are not always pathological because the emotionally healthy man does have some maternal identifications even though the dominant identification is with the parent of the same sex. In fact, it is this desirable balance of some feminine but predominantly masculine traits which makes him comfortable with the tenderness in his personality. However, in a marriage in which the wife is seeking symbiotic closeness and the husband holds out such promise because his feminine qualities are so great that they threaten his confidence in his masculinity, there can be conflict between the partners and within the individual in the partnership. We will have more to say about this when we discuss the defensive motivations for marriage—in this instance, the defense against homosexuality on the part of the husband. At this time, we wish to stress the imbalance that results in such situations because the wife feels betrayed as she finds that the husband is unable to fulfill the implied symbiotic promise; the husband feels bewildered because he cannot please without great threat to his tenuously held masculine position.

Mr. and Mrs. Edward exemplify the problems of premature marriage when the developmental tasks of adolescence have become too difficult because they are burdened by the incompletion of the developmental tasks of early childhood. Marriage, which is sought as a solution to these problems, compounds them further. By the time Mr. and Mrs. Edward come for counseling, they are in their middle twenties. They "fell in love" in high school when she was sixteen and he, seventeen. They knew immediately that they were "meant for each other" because they "clicked"; by this they mean that they had a perfect understanding without words. Each knew how the other felt at all times and each felt merged with and enveloped by the other. They were together almost constantly and they married as soon as Mr. Edward was graduated from high school and found a job. Mrs. Edward did not finish high school. She became pregnant at nineteen, and by now they have two young children. They have come for counseling because they are aware of problems which affect the children and because, despite constant bickering and attempts at separation, they cannot part.

In normal adolescent development, there is temporary regression and resumption of the separation-individuation struggle as well as temporary disequilibrium between the ego and the drives, which emerge in such great force after puberty. For Mr. and Mrs. Edward, there were stronger than usual symbiotic ties, indicating that the childhood phase of separation-individuation had not been adequately surmounted. They seized, too quickly, upon a solution to the tasks of adolescence which had become so burdensome for them. The social institution of marriage appeared to them, in its more obvious external manifestations, to be a solution to their psychological problems. Premarital counseling, if timely enough, might have prevented premature marriage and helped them with their discomfort in the increasing independence which has to be conquered in late adolescence. By the time they came for marital counseling, the task was more complex, but can be undertaken along the same theoretical lines nevertheless. Each partner is helped individually to master his and her own separation-individuation crisis in terms of the counselor's understanding of the individual life history and of the mother-child relationship in early childhood which prevented normal separation-individuation from taking place. A favorable outcome of such counseling would be the attainment of greater independence on the part of each spouse, thus freeing each to proceed to the point where the developmental opportunities of marriage and parenthood can be employed in a rewarding way.

The symbiotic mode of relating to another person is often the key to the understanding of problems which include poor gender identity and homosexuality. While these problems are not directly our subject, they do occur within marriage and make for difficulties which lead to disappointment and bewilderment similar to those already described. Treatment would follow along the same theoretical lines—freeing each individual in the marriage to proceed with his developmental thrust by helping him resolve the earlier developmental problems which impede the optimal employment of the developmental opportunities in the marriage. Thus, for example, if one of the partners in marriage consults a counselor because of homosexual tendencies or if such tendencies reveal themselves in the course of counseling which had been begun for other reasons, the counselor may know that one of several causes of homosexuality is incompletion of the separation-individuation phase. This is so because, at the symbiotic phase which precedes separation-individuation, the self and object are experienced as the same and gender distinctions are not yet made.

Finally, mention must be made of the marital difficulties which arise from fear of and, therefore, defense against symbiotic wishes. Here we note that the wish for symbiotic union may be feared and therefore defended against by its opposite. Thus, marriage counselors encounter problems which arise because the spouse complains of aloofness on the part of the partner. "He is cold and distant." "He seems not to need anyone." "She seems to push me away each time I approach her." These are indications to the counselor that the symbiosis is longed for but also feared. A kind of pseudo independence is established as a defense against the closeness which seems so dangerous because it threatens to obscure identity. This makes for a slightly more difficult technical problem in counseling because, if the counselor employs the transference as a therapeutic tool, the transference will also be cold, aloof, distant. The counselor must be able to tolerate and respect this as a defense against the symbiotic wish in order not to move in too quickly lest this arouse too much anxiety. It is not recommended that the longed-for closeness be gratified after the fear of it diminishes, but only that the counselor enable the spouse to understand it and, where the prognosis is favorable enough, to grow out of it.

We know that the phase of separation-individuation, which normally follows symbiosis in early child development, calls for attunement on the part of the mother to the child's growing independence. Whereas at the height of the symbiotic phase the mother must provide closeness, at the separation-individuation phase there must be readiness to permit distance and yet remain fixed and available so that the toddler may test out new skills within the security of being able to return for "refueling" when separation anxiety impels him toward mother again. Innumerable forays into the wider world and growing confidence in increasing skills coincide with the delineation of self from object. At such point, separation-individuation is first attained. The internal aspect of this process must again be emphasized. The child becomes separated and individuated in the sense that distinction between self representations and object representations within the ego is clear, whereas in the symbiotic phase it was blurred.

Marital problems which are based in inadequate completion of separation-individuation are not difficult to identify. Couples who separate and even divorce only to come together again and often to remarry may be living out the incompletion of the childhood developmental task. Perhaps because this is one of the most crucial of developmental phases, involving as it does the establishment of identity, it is never fully completed and, at each new thrust in development, must be reaffirmed. The developmental phase of marriage provides one of the several opportunities throughout life for such reaffirmation. Once again, after childhood and adolescence, a new opportunity for separation-individuation is offered within the context of a close relationship in which identity is reestablished and maintained. This new opportunity is provided by closeness in the intimacy of a relationship with a heterosexual partner of the same generation and dilutes the closeness to the primary family. Seen in this context, the counselor's familiarity with the external manifestations of separation-individuation problems in marital conflict is more profoundly elaborated. The weekly visits of the newlyweds to the parental homes, the frequent telephone conversations of the bride with her mother, the post-honeymoon quarrels about these, all become clearer if understood as back-and-forth movement away from the primary family analogous to the toddler's movement from and to mother in the original separation-individuation phase. In normal development within marriage, the establishment of new object relations with spouse and children takes over. Remaining within the analogy of the toddler-mother relationship, the parents of the newly married couple acquire a new role as "catalysts" of separation-individuation if they can tolerate this as a phase in their own life cycle as well. The developmental phase of the older couple with grown children is discussed more fully in Chapter X. Here, that part of their task which involves assisting the adult children in separation-individuation is stressed.

The developmental line of symbiosis and separation-individuation closely resembles that of object relations, but is not the same. Let us now consider that function of the ego which is termed *object relations*.

CHAPTER VI

Object Relations

WHAT is to be gained from review of the same problems from the developmental line of object relations that has not already been provided in our discussion of the symbiotic and separation-individuation developmental line? Perhaps this question is best answered by examining the Alfred case once again, adding this new dimension to our consideration of it. Mrs. Alfred's dominant psychosexual fixation is in the oral phase; from the ego side, she is largely symbiotically fixated and has not completed the separation-individuation crisis successfully. A second way of describing her ego development, consistent with Jacobson's thoughts about the fusion of self representations and object representations in the early months of life and their gradual differentiation as the personality becomes more structured, is that Mrs. Alfred's self representations and object representations are blurred. Adding to this a third factor of ego development—that of object relations—we would say that Mrs. Alfred's object relations are mainly on the need-gratifying level. What does this mean?

Hartmann proposes that there are three levels of object relations: primary narcissism, need-gratification, object constancy. Freud, Hartmann, Spitz, Mahler, and others are in substantial agreement that the phase of primary narcissism (autism) exists normally in the first three months of life. Clearly, fixations in and regressions to this first phase of object relations actually antedates the acquisition of meaningful object representations, and individuals at this level of development, when it is no longer phase-specific, are extremely disturbed, probably unable to function at large, and do not constitute the bulk of the married population.

When the infant emerges from the level of primary narcissism, he enters the level of need-gratification. In this process the infant acquires a more or less dim awareness that needs are fulfilled from without, but regards this "outside" as existing for purposes of his own gratification only. Obviously, this regard limits the relationship to the object to that of servant to his needs; she is good when she gratifies him and bad when he is frustrated. Persons at this level, when it is no longer phase-specific, can and do marry, and marital difficulties based in problems rooted in this level of object relations are frequently encountered. This is not to say that the person who regards a spouse as a need-gratifier is necessarily totally fixated at that level, although he or she may be. More often, however, the level of object relations fluctuates, so that there may be moments of regression as well as moments of recovery and return to a somewhat higher level. It must be remembered that, as is true of any phase of development that proceeds over a span of time, there is gradual emergence out of one phase into the next. Therefore, in the development of the infant, the concern with the external world would be less at the beginning of the level of need-gratification than when the need-gratification level begins to be superseded by the next higher level—object constancy. The theory could very well be refined by elaboration of subphases within these major phases of object relations so that we would then be in a position to describe early, middle, and late levels of primary narcissism, need-gratification, and object constancy. Analogous refinement has already been accomplished by Mahler's description of subphases of the separation-individuation phase.

Knowing Mrs. Alfred's symbiotic fixation, we may now add that, although she tends to regard the other person as part of herself and subservient to her needs, the ego function of perception nevertheless forces some awareness of an outside. That the external world exists primarily to serve her needs is descriptive of the level of object relations at which she functions, that is, of the manner in which she relates to others. This is a problem of fixation, of psychopathology. It is not a "selfish" attitude subject to correction by confrontation or by moralistic approaches such as lecturing on the rights of others. It is rather to be treated by techniques which include attempts at growth-promotion.

Understanding the factor of object relations as it applies to Mrs. Alfred also explains more fully why she and her husband are both dissatisfied, since no one can really exist solely to serve another. Even within the unity of the mother and infant in the symbiotic phase, it is only the infant who regards the mother as part of himself. The mother, having developed to adulthood, has a structured personality which, by definition, includes differentiation of self representations and object representations as well as object constancy. When it is phase-appropriate for the infant, the mother regresses temporarily, *but only partially,* to join with the infant in satisfying his symbiotic need. She may, at the same time, have other children whose phase-specific needs are different. For example, she may have an older child at the separation-individuation phase. If she is a "good enough" mother, she possesses the flexibility to relate to each child in accordance with different and often opposite needs; in addition, her relationship with her husband, an adult whose development is more or less completed as is hers, calls for relatedness different from that which she offers the children. Thus, that the mother is exclusively part of oneself is only the experience of the infant at the symbiotic phase and that she exists only to serve his needs is a factor of the need-gratifying level of object relations. It is this infant's eye view of the other person that Mrs. Alfred has not outgrown.

Mr. Alfred has reached a somewhat higher level of object relations than has his wife, perhaps having approached object constancy. His greater awareness that his children have needs different from his own suggests this. While he felt that he needed to leave his wife in search for gratifications which she could not offer, he realized at the same time that his children needed a father. Such small pieces of evidence, however, are not conclusive and the counselor should test them out further before making a final determination. A possibility which must be considered in such situations is that a father may, by employing identification and projection, feel that his children's needs coincide with his own. He may, for example, feel that they need more care and attention than is phase-specific for them, because these are his needs. In such instances, behavior which appears to be indicative of object constancy may be deceptive.

Object constancy, as defined by Hartmann, refers to the capacity to value the object for itself *independent of the state of need*. Whereas, at the need-gratification level it is the service which is valued; at the level of object constancy the other person has acquired value quite separate from the services which he may or may not perform. A useful analogy is that of a man who enters a restaurant because he is hungry. He orders from a waiter who remains anonymous because he is not concerned with the waiter as a person but only with his need for food and service. He is usually not even interested in the sex of the person who serves him and would accept the services of waiter or waitress with equal indifference to the person. The situation changes, however, if he frequents the same restaurant over a period of time and strikes up an intense friendship with the person who customarily serves him. Then he may find he is understood by that person, the manner of service becomes more personal, and if that particular waiter or waitress should be absent on a given day, he or she would be missed and the substitute would not be so highly regarded. There would ensue concern for the person's health, for the reason for the absence and other evidences of interest which tend to supersede the simple need for food.

This analogy illustrates the differences between and the transition from need-gratification to object constancy. In the case of the child, the mother, who at first is a need-gratifier only, gradually acquires value independent of the need. This desirable development in object relations comes about in the atmosphere of a predictable rhythm of frustration and gratification. Postponement of gratification is necessary to the growth process, but what happens in the period of postponement? How does the energy which originates in instinctual drive become available for ego building purposes when small amounts of frustration become tolerable? Hartmann has introduced the term *neutralization* to designate the process of making drive energy available to the ego. In the favorable mother-child situation which Hartmann terms the *average expectable environment*, memory of repeated experiences of gratification following frustration makes gratification predictable and enables the infant to wait for it. The desperate quality of urgent need subsides and, in the waiting period, the drive energy which is no longer necessary in full force undergoes transformation, or, as Hartmann puts it, becomes "neutralized" and thus is at the disposal of the ego instead of the id. While neutralized energy may be used by the ego for the development of many of its functions—speech, locomotion, and the like— here we are discussing the particular ego function of object relations. In this regard, neutralized energy which becomes available during the waiting process tends to be employed for the purpose of endowing the nurturing person with value which eventually becomes object constancy, that is, value which transcends need. Mother is no longer simply the servant who brings the food. This describes how the infant becomes capable of loving.

In marriage, the distinction between object constancy and fidelity is now understandable. Object constancy does not refer to fidelity in the legal, moral, or even physical sense; although a small aspect of it includes fidelity, object constancy is much broader than fidelity alone. It includes also the ability to tolerate absence because there is a constant, internalized object representation which therefore maintains a continuous relationship regardless of the physical presence of the other person. This latter is perhaps the best definition of constancy as it is used here—a constant, internalized object representation. Mrs. Alfred, although an adult, needs her mother's continued presence because internalization is inadequate. Absence makes the heart grow fonder when fondness thrives on refueling because object constancy has not been reached. This is normal for the child in the separation-individuation phase who is in the process of establishing object constancy. For the adult, feelings toward the other person remain more or less the same whether he is present or absent. This is a technical way of describing the ability to love. It seems that Mr. Alfred has at least some such potential. He may even love his wife more than he is consciously aware. Putting it to the counselor in terms of his not wanting to leave his children may be the only way in which he can verbalize this.

Further consideration of problems in marriage which arise out of fixation in the need-gratifying level clearly shows promiscuity as one of these. This symptom of inadequate development along the line of object relations is of major importance in marital counseling. Persons on the need-gratifying level of object relations can change partners so readily because the need is primary and the other person exists only to serve it. If one partner does not fulfill it, another will do. This is also a very good illustration of how psychosexual and physical maturation may, in the adult, have outpaced ego development, resulting in the search for sexual contact outside the context of object constancy. When promiscuity is understood in this way, the counselor will not condemn it or condone it or try to talk the patient out of it. He will know that no one can be expected to function beyond his psychological capacity and that the best treatment methods are those which are designed to enable the person to proceed in his development.

Another facet of object relations, and one which has an important bearing upon problems in marriage, is the concept of good and bad object. As already described, before the infant comes to the realization that both pleasurable and unpleasurable experiences are provided by the same person, his as yet hazy perception and his inability to distinguish between inside and outside lead him to regard the object as "good" and therefore as part of himself when the experience is pleasant and as "bad" and not-self when it is a frustrating experience. If good predominates and occurs in a predictable rhythm, the infant eventually comes to the realization that both "good" and "bad" objects are one person. He thus "fuses" the object, subsuming the "bad" under the "good," thereby becoming capable of tolerating less than perfection in one person. A man who has not successfully fused the good and bad objects may spend his life in unending search for the good one. The bad spouse, that is, the one who displeases at the moment, can be discarded in favor of another who is fantasied as good until the new one, too, disappoints by demonstrating human failings. Marriage counselors may be alert to the enthusiastic involvement with a new partner in a new romance which will succumb to disappointment in time. It is well, when such a pattern is suspected, to observe it over a period of time and to inquire about past involvements to see whether this is indeed the problem. Patients who have difficulties which stem from failure to have fused the good and bad objects are likely to be infantile in other aspects of their relationships as well and are therefore not difficult to identify.

The value of taking one's time to study the situation and of slowing down the patient who is eager for quick solution to the problem begins to emerge here. Many extramarital solutions, such as the search for the good object, really circumvent rather than solve, and many marriages would be saved by waiting and working things out more slowly. This does not mean that every marriage must and can be saved. There is a difference, however, between dissolution of a marriage after adequate study has determined that further development is not possible within it and its dissolution because a new partner seems to offer greater gratification to an individual whose inner structure remains the same. Numerous second and even third and fourth marriages fail in the same way as the first because nothing changes internally in the person who seeks solutions via external shifts. The sought-for good object can never be found.

Understanding of the multifaceted aspects of maturation and development enables us to see why would-be solutions which hold out promise of gratification in one area may disappoint in another. Mrs. Alfred seeks to gratify oral needs by overeating (and to counter them by dieting). In other words, she tries to gratify the instinctual drive in a primitive fashion. Two developmental factors remain frustrated: the symbiotic need which has extended as long beyond its phase-specific time as has the oral need, and the potential of the human being to form object relations, which has not developed beyond the level of need-gratification.

In similar fashion, Mr. Alfred's attempt to solve drive deprivation via sexual discharge has failed. At one time in his marriage, the absence of sexual gratification led him to have affairs with other women. The counselor may be drawn into an unnecessary dilemma about such solutions out of an understandable tendency to be sympathetic to the need. However, if the counselor realizes that the sexual need is only one factor in a complex of needs, he will know also why sexual discharge alone is usually not as satisfying as the person who seeks it hopes it will be. If it were, the person would probably not seek counseling. In every instance, the larger need is for a growth-promoting relationship. This follows from the thesis that development continues throughout life and that the failure of such development constitutes a frustration far greater than drive deprivation alone.

Since Mr. Alfred is not able to realize his developmental potential within his very constricting marriage, why not the solution of divorce and remarriage? The theory thus far expounded might suggest, logically, the solution of a new spouse with whom a higher level of object relations could be reached and maintained. This might indeed become the ultimate solution for someone like Mr. Alfred. It could only be undertaken with assurance, however, after a period of counseling which would reinforce his tendency toward the forward thrust of object constancy. The intermediary step in the counseling process should also include arriving at a thorough understanding of why he chose his present wife in the first place, because only through the awareness of the needs which keep him tied to her would he be truly free to choose whether he wishes to continue with her. Ultimately, the decision to terminate a marriage must rest with the patient alone. He is best equipped to make such a decision after a counseling experience which not only helps him understand himself and his needs better but offers him an opportunity to test his growth potential within the benign atmosphere of the counseling relationship. The counselor who has no need of his own to thwart growth by keeping the patient dependent upon him thus enables the patient to try his developmental wings. In

Mr. Alfred's case, such an experience would provide him with opportunity to choose whether his needs can be reasonably satisfied within his present marriage or whether a new marriage would better serve his further development and provide gratification of needs within the broad context described.

Persons who present the counselor with the solution of divorce at the outset of the counseling process are overlooking the unconscious ties to the present spouse. It is one of the counselor's many tasks, however, to keep this in mind and not be pressured into agreeing with hastily arrived-at solutions. Even after the problem is well understood and divorce is agreed upon as the only solution, the matter of severing the ties to the partner is of far greater importance than is usually considered. Second marriages, burdened by unresolved allegiances to the former partner, are so burdened because they have been entered into without psychological termination of the first marriage. Because of religious tradition, even those religions which sanction divorce do so reluctantly. Thus it has come about that religion participates in and thereby provides sociopsychological structure and meaning to marriage via ritual and ceremonial and continued sanction, but the termination of marriage is a cut-and-dried legal procedure which leaves the divorced persons with a bewildering and often unanticipated void. The more technical way of stating this is that object relations are built up in marriage, even in a bad marriage which must be terminated, and such ties are not severed by legal act. More usually understood and accepted is the period of mourning, after the death of a spouse, that must ensue before a new relationship can be undertaken. This is not simply a matter of time, although time is involved; it is a matter of the use of the time for the psychological process of terminating object relations. Again describing this in its most technical sense, it means gradual withdrawal of psychic energy from the internal representation of the lost object.

Only by this process does energy become available for reinvestment in a new object. The "work" of mourning is often insufficiently considered when divorce and remarriage are undertaken too quickly, although it is noticeable that persons in such situations often appear to be depressed over the loss of the recently divorced partner. Most adults who have married for other than purely need-gratifying purposes have some foothold in a level of object relations which precludes the ability to cast off the spouse as easily as the proverbial old shoe.

Mr. and Mrs. Frank have been unhappily married for twelve years. They spend most of their time together quarreling. Mr. Frank has been having an affair with another woman who seems to him to possess all of the virtues which his wife lacks. He describes each woman to the counselor in black and white terms. His wife is selfish, unfeminine, inconsiderate, insulting, unattractive, a frigid sex partner, and so on. His mistress is loving, thoughtful, attractive, interested in the same things as he, more pleasurable in sex, and so on. Here we see his "bad" object being contrasted with the "good" object. The counselor's first diagnostic thought is that there may be a defect in that the fusion of good and bad objects is lacking. However, Mr. Frank appears to function better in other areas; he has friends, colleagues, cares about his children, and works well. The counselor searches in the life history and does find some tentative evidence of early trauma in the first months of life. Reared in an upper middle-class family, Mr. Frank as an infant was excellently nourished by a series of different nurses and on a rigid schedule. Although fusion probably did take place, the fact that the real object changed so frequently leaves a quality of instability which emerges in the marital relationship, while business relationships and friendships are more readily controlled by reason. Even within the marital problem, there is evidence that a higher level of object relations was reached, although it often breaks down. The very fact that Mr. Frank seeks counseling indicates stronger ties there than appears, for, if that were not so, Mr. Frank would simply discard one woman after another. He cannot leave his family despite his conscious dissatisfaction. Looking beneath the surface, the counselor finds that this couple quarrels in the hope that each can force the other to give something more than his or her level of object relations actually permits. This means that each partner is at a need-gratifying level and wants his and her needs satisfied by the other. The level of object constancy, involving as it does the suspension of one's own needs at times, has not yet been attained by either partner. For Mr. Frank, because of the particular pathway toward regressive defusion of the good and bad objects, the attempted solution goes in a backward direction rather than toward further growth. The counselor's objective would be to remove the problems from the arena of marital struggle and then to try to help Mr. Frank, via the transference relationship, to fortify the tendency toward growth which had been weakened in infancy by the rapid changes in objects at a time when optimal developmental opportunity would have been better provided by consistency. The one-to-one relationship of the treatment process makes it possible for the counselor to employ such consistency to reinforce fusion. Then, the natural tendency toward further growth may enable him to use relationships outside treatment, that is, his marriage, for developmental rather than regressive purposes.

Mrs. Bernard, whose husband cannot tolerate her anxiety and her individual way of dealing with it, has attained a somewhat higher level of object relations than he. Evidence for this lies in his verbalizations. That his caustic remarks express aggression is apparent; slightly less apparent is his incapacity to understand that she has her own problem separate from his when she becomes anxious. Within the context of the matter of object relations, we would say that he is not altogether able to value the object independent of his own state of need. In Chapter V this was described as symbiotic need which makes it difficult for him to tolerate his wife's independent albeit neurotic functioning. Adding the dimension of object relations helps us also to question whether he functions at the need-gratification level all the time or only at moments of stress. This provides the counselor with a theoretical framework around which to explore other aspects of the marital relationship, work relationships, friendships, and the like. The counselor thus finds that, at other times, Mr. Bernard can give up an anticipated evening out if Mrs. Bernard is not well; that he does not always demand immediate gratification of sexual desire but takes his wife's readiness into account; that he can be understanding of her physical fatigue and lessened availability when one of the children has been ill. Although he has some difficulty in tolerating her involvement with the sick child, he is able to control himself better than when she has to scrub the floor. This provides interesting diagnostic distinction to the counselor's study of the problem because it is important to know that he is reasonable enough to be able to distinguish in importance the child's illness and the floor-scrubbing and to be more tolerant of the former. In this regard, the ability to identify with the child is useful; he is able to feel with the child that the mother is performing her maternal duties. The floor-scrubbing, on the other hand, seems altogether unnecessary to him because the floor is not dirty. Intellectual reasoning untempered by identification precludes empathy.

In another case, the counselor might discover that the father would be resentful of the mother's devotion to the sick child, thus indicating a lessened capacity to identify and more entrenched fixation in the need-gratifying level of object relations. Some men cannot bear their wives' involvement with a third person even when that person is his own child; others can be understanding of the child's needs but cannot think of their wives as having independent needs. These very common situations are often regarded observationally as the simple need for a mother on the part of the man. Such diagnostic thinking is a bit oversimplified; one must add the question "Which mother is needed?" It is often erroneously assumed that the wife represents the oedipal mother. If we bear in mind, however, that the oedipal relationship is on a rather high level of development in many respects, including object relations, then the men who are oedipally fixated would be able to value the object independent of their own state of need. Rivalry with one's son may very well represent failure of the resolution of the oedipal conflict, as everyone knows these days. Somewhat less well known is that it may also be a manifestation of pre-oedipal object relations and of need-gratification wishes which render the individual unable to take the needs of either wife or son into account.

The fluctuating quality of Mr. Bernard's object relations can be turned to therapeutic advantage. One can help him develop by supporting that which has been attained, namely, the ability to defer to the other person's needs at times, and to understand why he loses this ability in certain circumstances. The objective is to bring the lower level of functioning up to the higher level on more and more occasions; or, more technically, to close off the pathways that lead regressively to the need-gratifying level when there is stress. If the pressure of interrelated anxiety could be relieved, the marriage would no longer be the focal point for projection. The meaning of this statement is clearer now for, if Mr. Bernard's separation anxiety and Mrs. Bernard's anxiety about dirt were no longer to coincide and force each of them in a regressive direction, development would go forward.

The treatment for Mrs. Bernard with regard to object relations differs because her individual psychology is different. Psychosexually, she has reached the phallic-oedipal level, but regresses to the anal level when anxiety overwhelms her; in ego development, she has attained separation-individuation and a stable identity; on the object-relations scale, a fair level of object constancy has been reached. The latter conclusion is borne out by the observation that she does not demand need-gratification despite rather intense anxiety. Therefore, the counselor can rely on her ability to relate to form a stable transference which will constitute the backbone of treatment of her anxiety. Her level of development does not necessarily imply that she is more treatable than Mr. Bernard; the stability of her defenses may render her less treatable. We wish to stress that the treatment of each partner would take a different form because, although their individual problems converge at a certain point, their psychic structures are quite different.

Mr. and Mrs. Charles are able to function on a high level of object relations when their unconscious wishes and the defenses against the anxiety which these wishes produce do not impel them regressively. For Mrs. Charles, this means that her feeling of anatomical inadequacy stimulates tensions which cause her to disregard her husband's needs and wishes. Since the causes of her unconscious wish for a penis-baby are not evident, it will require careful diagnostic investigation to uncover them. Sometimes the wish for a baby is motivated by a need to have someone close and by the fantasy that a baby can fit that purpose; sometimes a woman will try to substitute baby for mother by means of an unconscious reversal of roles whereby the woman gratifies her own wish to be mothered by doing for the baby that which she would like done for herself. The counselor listens to Mrs. Charles as she talks about her wish for a child until it becomes clear that a baby represents a part of herself which, as a little girl, she thought was missing;

this thought has become unconscious. Such wishes, the residues of childhood misconceptions, result in difficulties in adult life because the logic of the childhood thought, since it is unconscious, fails to become integrated with adult logic. If Mrs. Charles were to become pregnant, she might enjoy a feeling of well-being while the baby is in reality part of her body, but would experience some difficulty in allowing the baby to separate from her—in the birth process, for example, or in the baby's increasing attempts at independence in his own developmental phases after birth. Since it is impossible for a person in the throes of an impelling wish to be able to foresee the future difficulties, the counselor should know that Mrs. Charles's solution would not be as satisfying as she thinks and that, even with a child, her basic discontent would remain.

Since Mrs. Charles is not yet pregnant at the time that she comes for counseling, but presents the problem of her wish for a baby as creating marital difficulty, it is worthwhile examining the effect of the overpowering wish on her otherwise well-developed level of object relations. Because unconscious wishes brook neither refusal nor even delay in their demand for fulfillment, this rather reasonable young woman musters argument in favor of a desire of which she is not really aware. The very wish itself is unconsciously altered so that it sounds quite reasonable—she is married and wants to start a family. The only clue to the counselor that this demand is motivated by a little girl's wish for a penis is the urgency and the incongruous disregard of her husband's wishes in a matter which should be a jointly desired fulfillment of their marriage. This illustrates how a higher level of object relations can regress, partially, to the level of need-gratification when the pressure of an unconscious wish is felt.

On Mr. Charles's part, there is well-intentioned conscious desire to make his marriage work. Having failed in his first marriage, he applies himself sincerely and diligently to pleasing Mrs. Charles, and, for the most part, he succeeds. There may even be an exaggerated wish to please which sometimes operates in too much disregard for his own wishes. However, this does not seem to be more than mildly masochistic and might not in itself cause severe problems to Mr. Charles or to the marriage. What does provide a serious threat is the clash between Mrs. Charles's insistence upon a baby now and Mr. Charles's equally firm insistence that it can wait. A matter which should constitute a major milestone of development in marriage—movement toward the developmental phase of parenthood—has become a point of contention between the partners. On Mrs. Charles's part, her usually good level of object relations is not operative in this one respect; for Mr. Charles, the threat to his masculinity of his wife's demand that he provide her with a penis-baby sets in motion defensive behavior which requires that he forestall fantasied injury. Thus, the need of Mrs. Charles and the defense of Mr. Charles both become so overriding that each is blinded to the situation of the other.

Once the counselor understands the nature of the clash between these two partners, it becomes possible to help them. It requires of the counselor a stance of neutrality, which, in this case, means not being swayed by the arguments on either side. The counseling procedure per se is directed toward enabling each spouse to gain insight that the difficulty is not a joint but an individual one. Mr. Charles's castration anxiety and Mrs. Charles's wish for a penis converge and create a marital problem. However, they originate in childhood, and it may therefore be said that, although they burden the marriage, they have nothing to do with it. If the counseling process enables them to understand that exactly, it will have accomplished a great deal. While resolution of the basic problem in each partner may require psychoanalytic treatment in depth, counseling can help them cease projecting, release the potential for their highest levels of object relations to become operative, and lead them into depth therapy if they so desire. It may be added that psychoanalytic therapy is recommended, not because Mr. and Mrs. Charles are so emotionally disturbed but because, on the contrary, they have such excellent potential that they would benefit greatly from it. This may be contrasted with the recommendation for Mr. and Mrs. Alfred. For them, because of their more fragile structures, more limited forms of treatment are indicated.

In the treatment process, the level of object relations is of crucial importance in the establishment of a transference and working alliance with the therapist. Transference refers to the repetition of past object relations projected on the therapist in the treatment situation; it is extremely useful in reconstructing and working through past relationships. Working alliance refers to the real relationship with the therapist and includes the ability to identify with him in his treatment objectives. The value of both in the treatment process cannot be overstressed. Since they depend so much upon the level of object relations, this becomes the single factor, above all others, upon which prognosis may be based.

For Mr. and Mrs. David, the problem revolves around another aspect of object relations not yet described. This entails the distinction between the parental figure in the pre-oedipal and oedipal phases. The residual relationship, as in the Bernard case, with the parent of early childhood cannot be understood by means of the oversimplified concept of "mother fixation" or "father fixation." In an evaluation of the problem, the counselor must always keep in mind, "Mother or father as of when?", for the purpose of providing a framework around which to listen to the patient for answers. Clues will be provided by what the patient says and especially by how the patient relates to the counselor. In the pre-oedipal phase, when the child is more dependent upon the omnipotently perceived parent, the relationship is more passive than it is in the oedipal phase when it shifts to a more active, assertive mode. So far as the ego is concerned, its tasks in the oedipal phase are little short of stupendous and it must be very strong indeed. This is why neurotics, with relatively strong and intact egos, founder on the oedipal conflict nevertheless. The best opportunity for the successful mastery of the oedipus is provided by the optimal equipment which earlier development makes possible, for the power of both sexual and aggressive drives emerge in full force and must be mastered. For the boy, the former primarily maternal mother becomes a sexual object; for the girl, the mother upon whom she depended for gratification of passive needs becomes a rival. The oedipal task, for both sexes, is so demanding because, no sooner does it reach its developmental aim—shift from passive relationship to pre-oedipal object to active sexual and competitive relationship to oedipal objects—than it has to be postponed and ultimately overcome in the course of further development. The task of postponement, in particular, involves supreme exercise of the ability to tolerate frustration, to neutralize both libidinal and aggressive drives, and to maintain the intactness of the fused "good" and "bad" object so that the "good" predominates. Since all of this takes place within the first five years of life, it is apparent how crucially important is the building of adequate object relations in preparation for the oedipal struggle. Without object constancy and the climate of benign parents, the child becomes hopelessly overpowered by libidinous and aggressive wishes with which he cannot cope in a hostile environment. In the sense in which we are discussing object relations, the environment includes not only the real parents, as they are, but also their internalized representations. It follows from this definition that, even though the parents may in reality be "nice" to the child in the oedipal phase, the child's concept of them is derived from earlier experiences which have become internalized. Difficulty ensues in the oedipal phase, as well as at other phases, when less than benign object representations are reinforced in a negative direction by the child's projection of his own hostile wishes upon the parents. While such projection is normal, it has less impact if the reality does not support it.

Much of the problem between Mr. and Mrs. David is caused by his behavior lending an aura of reality to her fantasy. His fatherly attitude toward her maintains in her unconscious the fiction that he *is* the father she loved as a little girl. While both partners are bewildered by their sexual difficulties, the counselor need not be equally bewildered if he understands his task as enabling each of them to develop beyond the oedipal object relationships. The counseling task with Mr. David is a very difficult one and may entail skilled psychoanalytic psychotherapy or psychoanalysis per se to help him overcome the developmental trauma of the early loss of his father. Loss of a parent and particularly of the parent of the same sex before the final resolution of the oedipal conflict in adolescence prevents completion of this vital developmental task.

For Mrs. David, if further exploration corroborates the assumption that her early object relations developed favorably, the counselor can depend upon a good ability to form a transference and to work with him toward the resolution of her problem. The usual first step which we have been advocating is applicable here: help each partner to the understanding that the problem is based in the unique vicissitudes of his or her own development rather than in the problems of the partner or in the marriage per se. Sometimes, this procedure alone enables development within the marriage to proceed.

Marriage is a developmental phase in the life cycle. That aspect of marriage which promotes continued development of higher levels of object relations is best served when the partners enter marriage having proceeded beyond the level of need-gratification in early life. This provides them with the fundamental equipment needed to deal with another person in recognition of needs which differ from one's own. Marriage involves both moments of convergence of the partners' needs which they then mutually gratify, and moments when individual needs do not coincide. It is at time of divergence that the level of object relations not only is put to the test but is also provided with an opportunity to develop further. This is another way of stating also that the best chances for successful marriage exist when the partners bring a certain minimum of favorable childhood development to it. When this is not so, the counseling task is far more difficult because fundamental psychological shortcomings then have to be remedied before levels of object constancy that make marriage workable can be attained. When it is so, however, the ever-increasing opportunities for new and higher levels of object relations in marriage possess an almost infinite quality because the daily experience of living with and taking into account the needs of another duplicates in some respects the original developmental phase in which the infant gradually comes to love and value the other person. It has been observed that, in marriages that endure over a period of years, love deepens. This is so because of the new opportunities which have been employed in the development of object relations, that is, in deploying energy from need-gratification toward endowing the loved one with value. Such process attains even greater importance as the next stage, parenthood, is reached, and makes it possible for love to extend to the new family members.

CHAPTER VII

Internalization

WHEN the counselor encounters an individual in the consulting room, the manifest appearance of his problem may be likened to the appearance of the performer on a stage. Although illuminated by a dozen spotlights, each contributing its own tones, only the convergence of light upon him in its combined effect is visible. The complexity of human psychology is such that each of the many maturational and developmental factors has to be considered separately for the counselor to be able to evaluate the effect of each upon the whole. While the lighting engineer visualizes the effect that he wishes to produce and selects each light for its individual contribution, the counselor or therapist works in reverse, viewing the end result and then trying to identify the components. Such tracking down of the separate but often parallel factors in individual development is never easy, but is made considerably more so by a thorough knowledge of them.

Previously, we used phrases such as "self representations and object representations" and "internalization" because the concepts which they represent are involved in the processes whereby object relations are built up. Now, let us examine these concepts in greater detail. While most of the discussion is concerned with that process of internalization known as identification, it is useful to know that identification is but one of several processes of internalization, the principal others being introjection and incorporation. Internalization is the process of making part of oneself that which once was external. In the beginning of life, this is likely to be rather primitive and total. In the oral phase, the capacity to select and abstract is absent and the desire literally to ingest via the mouth is dominant. The tendency is to *introject*, that is, to internalize that which appears desirable. (The counter tendency, to *project*, is the infant's way of dealing with whatever is undesirable.) Obviously, introjection (and projection) is possible only when what belongs outside and what belongs inside is not yet clear. Another process of internalization, *incorporation*, is not the literal swallowing performed under the direction of the instinctual drive but the ego aspect of the same phenomenon; not literal objects but attitudes are ingested. Via incorporation, the child makes part of himself the parental admonitions regarding behavior.

Although identification is often used as if it were synonymous with internalization and although such usage is not incorrect, accuracy demands that it be borne in mind that internalization is the generic term and identification is subsumed under it. *Identification* may be defined as the internalization of aspects of another person—qualities, mannerisms, characteristics, values—which are admired and desired as one's own. They become part of the self by means of creating a mental representation in the ego. As is true for every aspect of development, there are gradations in identification processes and the early ones—the precursors of true identification, we might say—are not yet fully internalized. Imitation is the earliest forerunner of identification; it replicates the object in much the same way as would a camera, simply copying what is outside oneself. Only as structuralization of the personality proceeds does a more complex and sophisticated procedure replace imitation. As the ability to distinguish outside from inside is perfected and as the ego becomes capable of selecting abstract characteristics in addition to the simple mannerisms which it had heretofore copied, identification begins to consist of something more like a painting than a photograph in that not necessarily everything is imitated; the individual may then become *like* the object in certain respects, but retains individual characteristics and blends these together with those he adopts from the other person, making something new and uniquely his own out of them. He is no longer in danger of becoming totally *the same* as the object.

This analogy may be used to distinguish identification as a normal process of development from the emergency measure which it sometimes is. Where identification takes place at an ongoing, relatively unpressured pace, it offers the possibility of being integrated into the developing personality structure. Leisure permits selectivity and creativity. As a defense, however, option is sacrificed and the existing structure becomes overwhelmed by the abruptly introduced identification instead of having the opportunity to integrate it. The autonomous characteristics of the individual cannot be enhanced, as in normal identification, but become subverted to the defensive effort.

Historically, the defensive aspect of identification was known first; it was only later in the development of psychoanalytic theory that the normal process of identification was understood as essential in the development of the individual. As a defense, it can be used to make it possible for the person to endure the sudden loss of an important object. It replaces the lost external object with an internal one—hence, identification. The case of Mr. David illustrates how this deprives the process of its developmental quality. Since the death of his father occurred when Mr. David was twelve years old, it is assumed that, if former development proceeded well enough, psychic structure was well established. Nevertheless, the trauma was so great that Mr. David had to *become* his father to a pathological degree to cope with the loss. Such "coping" does not really deal with the loss, because, via identification, the object survives within. Had his father lived longer, the more leisurely and normal process of identification and final affirmation of gender identity in later adolescence would have been possible for Mr. David. The more fortunate adolescent boy, whose father exists in reality for him to emulate as he grows to adulthood, has better developmental opportunity. He can employ identification to become like his father insofar as some of his father's qualities serve his development, and he can retain his own uniqueness. Mr. David was also deprived of the normal adolescent opportunity to work out his oedipal rivalry because, for this too, the boy needs the presence of a benign and understanding father. For Mr. David, it became necessary to repress competitive wishes, and excessive identification served the additional purpose of aiding such repression. Instead of becoming *like* his father, he *became* his father to a pathological degree.

Although processes of internalization were discovered and described in psychoanalytic theory before ego psychology, in this aspect of theory as well, ego psychology provides added dimension. To the description of how neutralization of drive energy promotes the formation of object relations (Chapter VI), we can now add that gradual internalization of the object begins in the same way. Memory traces of the gratifying experience which makes waiting possible and initiates neutralization includes memory of the at first dimly perceived external object and provides the basis for the gradual establishment of stable object representations. With the differentiation of self representations and object representations, a sense of personal identity comes into being. At the same time, there can be security in the absence of the object because the internal representation remains. Children sometimes wonder whether persons or things exist when they are not present. For the child before internalization has taken place, they exist only when he sees them. "Out of sight, out of mind" means that there is no internal representation in the mind. Another example of this phenomenon is drawn from this same stage of life. The child who fears the dark room does the following:

1. He peoples the unseen and unseeable darkness with his own anxious fantasies because

2. he is unable to project into the darkness an image of a benign and loving mother because

3. he does not contain such image in his own mind and, therefore

4. he needs his actual mother with him.

This may also be seen in the case of Mrs. Alfred who has to have her mother with her all of the time or else suffer unbearable anxiety; mother does not exist when she is not visible.

Hartmann puts this theoretical concept in bolder terms: the greater the degree of internalization, the more independent of the environment does the organism become. In this sense, Mrs. Alfred does not have sufficient internalization for independence. An analogy may be found in the process whereby one learns how to drive a car. The beginner, at the outset, cannot get into the car and drive away. He requires the actual physical presence of the instructor. It is only when his skill and confidence have increased to the point where he no longer needs the instructor with him that one might say that he has internalized the teachings and no longer needs the physical presence of the whole object. Thus, he has become independent of the environment. This analogy also illustrates the concept of partial or selective identification. The new driver has not *become* the instructor, but has adopted that aspect of the other person which he wishes to make part of himself. It is not intended to convey, however, that identification is as deliberate and conscious a process as learning to drive a car. Both types of identification, the defensive pathogenic type and the normal selective type, take place outside the individual's awareness. In the latter, however, although the choice is unconscious, there is nevertheless the already-mentioned quality of volition. Married couples who live together for a long time and who tend to take on one another's characteristics do not dislike having had this happen to them.

One of the most vital aspects of internalization is its role in the establishment of that part of the psychic structure known as the superego. This is the part of the personality which contains the moral, ethical, and behavioral standards of the individual. It is the last structure to be formed in the developmental process, and in some respects the most complex and least understood. The infant does not arrive into the world as a socialized human being who is responsible for his own conduct; it takes many years to reach that point. At first he is incapable of abiding by society's rules. Reasonable parents introduce society's demands gradually and at phase-specific times. The infant's first major experience in curbing instinctual demand to conform with external prohibition occurs in the weaning process. However, if weaning is imposed when orality is on the wane, he accepts socialization in this regard and the way is paved for the next juxtaposition of civilization against instinctual drive—toilet training. In learning how to oppose his own drives in the interest of maintaining object relations the child incorporates the parental prohibitions and thus makes them his own. Such gradual incorporation in the early years provides the building blocks out of which the superego will be formed in the oedipal and post-oedipal phases. Until that time, however, they remain disparate entities, only partially internalized and not yet mortared into the cohesive structure that the superego later becomes. At these pre-oedipal stages of superego formation, partially internalized parental values and prohibitions are, for want of a better term, usually referred to as "precursors" of the superego. As such, they are not yet competent to perform regulatory functions with regard to behavior and they rely heavily upon reinforcement from without. The child, at this stage of development, knows the rules because the parents have promulgated them, but lacks fully established capacity for inner enforcement. The importance of understanding this interim stage of superego formation is made clear when we look at the kind of adult with whom the marriage counselor sometimes has to deal who has not proceeded in superego formation. Such a person may demonstrate certain delinquent characteristics. A man may steal small things from his employer if he thinks he will not be caught; he may lie to his wife about his whereabouts and only worry about being found out. A woman may "steal" from her household money or, as in many jokes, from her husband's trousers pocket while he is asleep. These kinds of behavior are not criminal in the sense that the behavior of the person with defective, psychopathic structure is. The latter superego defect is more easily diagnosed, but more difficult to treat. The more usual kind of superego defect which is likely to come to the attention of the marriage counselor is the one described and is the result of incompletion of development. Such persons are still more afraid of external detection than of internalized strictures. The counselor may put it to himself in the form of a question: "Which does he fear, his conscience or the policeman?" If he fears the policeman, then he does not have a fully structured superego with internalized self-regulation.

Therapists are generally rather familiar with another type of shortcoming in superego formation—the oversevere or self-punitive superego. While the psychopath has too little superego, and the kind of person described above has an incompletely formed superego, the individual with an oversevere superego usually suffers from having developed a premature structure. In other words, it is not only a quantitative matter of too much, but also too soon. Premature superego development most often comes about when parental strictures are too harsh, but it can also result from the opposite. Overpermissive parents and educators leave the child at the mercy of instinctual demands with which he is unable to cope and sometimes he establishes a rather harsh structure with which to curb himself. So we may encounter the oversevere superego which is the result of incorporation of harsh parental prohibitions; the type which is the result of too lenient parental control; and one other, similar to the latter, which is familiar in neurosis and which results from defensive attempt to deal with the drives. Therapeutic measures for dealing with the problem of oversevere superego logically direct themselves toward establishing greater leniency. While this is not incorrect, it is often oversimplified because it is based on the somewhat fallacious idea that oversevere means *too much*. If the developmental feature of *too soon* is taken into account as well, the matter becomes more complex. Then, the counselor or therapist must also consider the question of *why too soon,* that is, the place of the harsh structure in the totality of development. Counselors are lately encountering more and more young adults who are the products of overpermissive upbringing and therefore the incompletely developed or prematurely developed superego comes into therapeutic prominence.

The greater freedom of premarital sex that is now accepted brings difficulty to those adolescents and young adults whose uneven development renders them inadequately prepared to encompass the experience and to integrate it into their growth. Bewildered young persons of both sexes present themselves for treatment with vague distress which they are unable to define. One cause of this distress is that ego and superego development have not kept pace with the drives, and the superego has not developed to the point where it can perform regulatory functions. Where this incomplete development has resulted in an inadequately internalized and structured superego, the individual's attitude toward the counselor takes the form of an unexpressed wish to be curbed. The counselor may keep in mind, "He wants me to stop him because he needs external policing, that is, he does not have an internalized superego and looks to someone on the outside to perform this curbing function for him." This in no way implies that the counselor should comply with the wish to be prohibited because such a technique would not be growth-promoting. However, if he understands the problem in this way, the counselor can then go on to understand the balance between ego and superego underdevelopment and to devise therapeutic methods for the promotion of such functions as judgment, choice, decision on the part of the ego, and self-regulation on the part of the superego. The goal would be to enable the individual to regulate his own behavior in his best interests; these interests include avoiding experiences which promote more disintegration. It is in this context that premarital and extramarital sex, as well as other forms of behavior which make the individual uncomfortable, must be discussed. The counselor who has to deal so much with extramarital escapades will be most effective if he does not accept at face value the individual's conscious declarations concerning gratification, but lends himself to exploring the growth-promoting or growth-inhibiting qualities in the behavior. Where the problem is rooted in inadequate internalization, the most highly skilled counseling will be directed toward enabling internalization to proceed. While this usually involves a certain degree of selective identification with the therapist, such process is not to be confused with the provision of a so-called corrective emotional experience. The concept of *corrective emotional experience* is based upon a misunderstanding of internalization. The patient, especially the adult patient, never presents himself as a "clean slate" ready to absorb a new experience with a new person, but as one already possessed of a personality which includes self representations and object representations and ego and superego development. If these include faulty, inadequate, or incomplete internalization, the therapeutic task is that of *correction* of already established internalizations and not simply of superimposing new ones via an experience with the counselor. While the therapeutic encounter *is* an experience, it is an experience more in getting to know oneself than in internalizing the values of the counselor. Nevertheless, when the "slate" becomes cleaner, that is, when negative and distorted self and object representations are corrected and faulty identifications are revised, the therapeutic process, like any profound experience with another person, does result in a certain amount of selective identification.

The problems caused by overrigid, prematurely formed superego may be on the increase because there has been this excessively permissive upbringing in the last twenty-odd years. The person who forms such a structure presents himself as exceedingly harsh in his self-judgment. For treatment purposes, it is necessary diagnostically to distinguish him from the person with an oversevere superego which has the purpose of defense. The latter, of which Mrs. Bernard is an example, has a fairly well-developed ego, but needs a harsh superego nevertheless because the drive threatens to break through. The former type is also threatened by the drives, of course, but has developed a premature and overly harsh superego principally as a substitute for parental control because, at the phase-specific time, such parental control was absent. It is as though such persons are "loved" by the superego which watches over them. This arrangement succeeds very poorly. It is like being loved by one's jailer who administers daily punishment lest there be any wrongdoing. Sometimes such persons are described as masochistic, but we find it more useful clinically to indicate the developmental defect in this kind of harsh self-judgment. To clarify further the difference between this type of person and Mrs. Bernard, we might say that Mrs. Bernard has internalized the strict prohibitions of her mother with regard to cleanliness and reverts to them in moments of stress, whereas the overpermissively reared person has had nothing to internalize and thus has constructed a false and shaky structure which does not operate well for him. Such persons are sometimes aware that they are unable to make wise choices about courses of action, often act anyway, and become severely self-critical or severely anxious.

Mrs. George, whose mother died when she was thirteen, was left completely to her own devices by her grief-stricken father. While her schoolmates had to be home at a definite hour at night, she had no curfew. After staying out until three o'clock several mornings, she became so terror-stricken that she told her friends that she had to be home at eight o'clock every evening, thus providing herself with a feeling of being protected by setting a stricter curfew than her friends had. When she began to have sexual relationships some years later, she was similarly terrified. By the time she married, she became frigid in sex, thus once again providing herself with an overly strict and inappropriate "protection." This is an arrangement which cannot be undone simply by the counselor's permissiveness, because it is easy to see, in this case, that permission from without will not alter the internalized aspect of the problem. It is better for the counselor to avoid permissiveness altogether and this is made simple if he bears in mind that to be nonjudgmental, which is helpful, is not the same as to be permissive, which is frightening.

Mrs. Bernard's case illustrates so well the classic problem of the harsh superego in neurosis that it merits elaboration. When she is compelled to scrub the floor she is really engaged in a desperate attempt to combat instinctual wish with superego prohibition. The element of penance and propitiation is also apparent here because she literally sentences herself to hard labor. Understanding the internalized aspect of superego development in Mrs. Bernard, its origin in identification with an overly clean mother in the toilet-training period, and its use against anxiety-evoking situations in the present shows also how Mr. Bernard's involvement is so ineffectual. It is nothing that Mrs. Bernard can control and the counselor helps both partners best by helping Mr. Bernard stay out of it. When Mrs. Bernard's internal equilibrium is altered therapeutically, she will relax about cleanliness. More technically stated, the oversevere superego will be replaced by a more benign one when she is better able to cope with her instinctual wishes with lessened anxiety.

Probably one of the most important and least understood functions of the superego is its role in the maintenance of identity. This is particularly pertinent in a study of marriage and warrants reemphasis because marriage requires the maintenance of identity within a life-context of "togetherness." Also, identity is established by the gradual differentiation of self representations from object representations in the early years of life and by the completion of the separation-individuation crisis resulting in "psychological birth." Because life, and especially married life, involves closeness with others and this includes the constant stimulation of regressive wishes for symbiotic union, identity is not really once and for all established, but requires reaffirmation and maintenance. We have seen how the adolescent struggles overtly for this. Many marital struggles contain similar elements of defiance and overemphasis upon difference, inappropriate to the real situation, but necessary in the individual's economy if understood as founded upon the struggle to maintain identity. If, however, a benign and well-structured superego has developed out of healthy identification with the parent of the same sex, then one's sense of well-being reflects a stable identity which includes firmly established gender identity. It is this aspect of the superego—the following in the footsteps of the parent in his or her gender role that maintains and guards identity in marriage. Many marital quarrels about who should wash the dishes and who should feed the baby, and the like, are based upon uncertainty in gender identity. While modern living appears to blur the distinction between man and woman because both may perform certain acts with equal efficiency, the internalized distinction should remain clear. The threats to masculinity by some wives' insistence upon participation by the husband in household tasks is an internal threat. There is much talk these days about men being psychologically castrated by the spouse or even by society, but a man whose masculinity is firmly established and maintained by a benign identification with his father who had, in the developmental years, accepted and encouraged such identification, cannot have his masculinity impaired from without.

In favorable circumstances, the marital situation offers, among its developmental opportunities, the major one of reaffirmation of gender identity. The self images of male and female are emphasized by entering into the marital state. The roles of man and woman are lived out and become even more thoroughly reaffirmed in the roles of father and mother. A man can only feel more masculine when he has a woman to love, provide for, engage in marital relations with, and produce children by. There is, similarly, no other arrangement which can provide a woman with better opportunities to develop her feminine role in love, tenderness, maternity. Cross-identifications are also enhanced within the security of fixed identification. A man's tender qualities find more secure expression when his masculinity is secure. A woman may work, engage in intellectual pursuits, drive a car, and otherwise invade what used to be a "man's world" without losing her femininity. Those couples who do begin to resemble one another take on this cross-identification when there is lessened risk of loss of individual identity. What happens in marital counseling when some of these identifications fail?

Mr. and Mrs. Harold were in their forties and had adolescent children when they came for counseling. Mr. Harold's overt functioning had always appeared to be excellent until his business failed. Before that, the Harolds appeared to be the typical middle-class suburban family with home, car, college in the offing for the children, friends, and community involvement. Upon the failure of the business it became evident that all had been held together by this one thin thread, that is, by external trappings in lieu of internalization and stable identity. Having lost his role as businessman and family provider, Mr. Harold missed inner conviction of identity. Mrs. Harold began to quarrel with him and to try to force him to continue to function by embarking upon another business venture without realizing that all this was beyond his psychological capacity at the time. The counselor realized that there must have been serious failure in completion of superego development and that this developmental defect had not been detected earlier because it was not the usual kind which simply results in delinquency and brings the individual into conflict with the law. There had been sufficient opportunity, in sharp business practices, to engage in semidelinquent behavior while still remaining within the letter of the law. In fact, society rewarded this activity with financial success. Mr. Harold had never functioned independently in the sense of having to make his way in the world because he had entered the family business when he completed high school. It was because of this protective setting that his inadequate sense of identity, the incompletion of the development of his superego, and the absence of conviction about his masculinity had not emerged sooner. When the business failed, the inner structure could not maintain him.

This is an exceedingly complex situation with deep pathology and one might well question why such depth problems are included in a book on marital counseling. Marital counseling was the only avenue by which this couple could approach help for their problems. It was the quarreling which led them, understandably, to the counselor. Thus, although the problems are of a much deeper nature, the counselor does well to begin where the patients see the problem and to lead them to further help as they become able to accept it. In very many situations, the interactional disquiet in the marriage provides the wedge toward insight into the more profound pathology. The counselor must be prepared, when such insight is attained, to treat the problem or to make an appropriate referral.

Many less severe problems of internalization, treatable by the marriage counselor, contain within them confusion about gender identity. One is the use of marriage by the latent homosexual as a defense, that is, as protection against the outbreak of homosexual wishes. He is similar to the Don Juan character, who has been described in the psychoanalytic literature, compelled to engage in endless heterosexual conquest to prevent homosexual urges from emerging. In part, such uncertainty about gender identity entered into Mr. Bernard's tendency to deal so rigidly with Mrs. Bernard's need to clean house. He could neither tolerate the temptation to pitch in and help, nor feel comfortable about remaining aloof from it. Mr. David, on the other hand, had established a rather solid gender identity out of his identification with his father, but at too high a price. Many wives such as Mrs. Charles and Mrs. David, have lived all their lives with great confusion about and resentment at being girls and bring to their marriages a tendency to reject femininity.

Looking more closely at Mrs. David in this regard, her girlish qualities, which appear so endearing, reflect a failure of internalization. She continues to be her Daddy's little girl. This poses the question of what happened, or what failed to happen, when she was truly a little girl. To reply to this question within the language and thought of the concept of internalization and its processes, one would say that the self representations—those perceptions of the self which reside within the ego—endow Mrs. David with an image of herself as a child. Why, as she grew older, did this self-image not alter with altering self-perceptions? One answer is that the goal of womanhood was not presented to her as desirable because her mother did not enjoy her own femininity. The solution which Mrs. David employs is, in reality, not a solution, but something more in the nature of a fixation. She unconsciously refuses to grow up to be a woman, assuming erroneously thereby that remaining a little girl is a matter of choice which obviates the problem of feminine identification with which she was faced in childhood.

The counseling problem, in such cases, is not very difficult, especially where the pathology is not too great. The task is to help the patient clarify and understand gender identity. Orientation in the developmental point of view with regard to identity includes, for the counselor, the conviction that each individual wishes to be what he or she really is and to enjoy a comfortable self-image.

CHAPTER VIII

Anxiety and Defense
in Marriage and Divorce

NOT only psychologists, but even poets, allude to the comfort and security of the fetal state when the organism experiences no tension. In the state after birth, the relaxation of peaceful sleep sometimes approximates fetal bliss. In waking life, the fortunate individual experiences optimal moments of peace when the three components of his psychic structure—id, ego, and superego—are in harmony. This occurs when the ego succeeds in arranging an activity which gratifies instinctual striving to conform both with the demands of reality and with the approval of the superego. Such is the way that instinctual tension is discharged without anxiety. Even the strongest and most developed ego cannot succeed in making such excellent arrangements all of the time, and so anxiety is a part of living, to be borne by all of us some of the time.

By definition, anxiety is an uncomfortable affective state. How uncomfortable depends not only upon its quantity but upon what devices the individual has learned to employ to cope with it and how well these devices work. In psychoanalytic terminology, the characteristic ways in which an individual deals with anxiety is called *defense*. Defense shares with other aspects of psychological development the feature of originating in the early, formative years of life. By the time adulthood is reached, these defensive arrangements are usually fixed, unconscious, and automatic. An important part of the adult personality, therefore, is characterized by the defensive structure; this, in turn, is determined by how early and under what conditions anxiety was experienced and with what success it was coped with in infancy and childhood. Since it is the ego that experiences and deals with anxiety, the young infant, with a relatively undeveloped ego, subjected to trauma, will be able to adopt only the most primitive and ineffectual defenses. The simplest example of a primitive defense mechanism is *denial*. By denying its existence, the individual ignores that which makes him anxious. Behaviorally, this is observable in young infants who turn their heads away or close their eyes to that which is disturbing. While such device is normal in the infant, an older child or adult who continues this means of dealing with unpleasant reality without having developed more sophisticated defenses is in great psychological difficulty. Because reality is so disturbing to him, in denying it, he fails to find effective ways of dealing with it. It is like closing one's eyes and plunging across the street at a busy intersection. One may, by good fortune, arrive safely at the other side, but it cannot be said that this was negotiated by an efficiently functioning ego.

As the ego develops and becomes stronger in its role of mediator between inner demands and outer reality, more complex and efficient mechanisms of defense come into play. We have already spoken of *introjection* and *projection* which, although perhaps a notch beyond *denial,* are also not very effective defenses because of the confusion between inside and outside. In the middle range lie a number of defense mechanisms familiar in the psychoanalytic literature, such as *reaction-formation, isolation, undoing, regression,* and others. Operatively, such mechanisms of defense are seen in combination rather than separately, and it takes a moderate amount of clinical sophistication for the counselor to learn to identify them. The best known of the mechanisms of defense, *repression,* is sometimes the least understood because of the histori-

cal accident of its discovery. When Freud first began his work
on hysteria, he used the term *repression* synonymously with
defense; some years later, he revised his view, as he began to
understand that repression is a particular type of defense—
one among several. Another erroneous thought which persists
beyond its time is that all repression is harmful to the individual. This fallacy also arises out of Freud's earliest work with
hysteria which was then thought to be caused by repressed
traumatic memories. Such was the simplicity of early psychoanalysis, which evidences itself also in the conclusion that,
with the recovery of such memories, cure is accomplished.

Today, matters are no longer so simple, and there are three
major reasons for this. The first is that we have come to regard repression as not always being pathological but having
also the normal function of keeping our minds "in order" in
the sense that it keeps out of consciousness that which would
be burdensome to know. In fact, one of the problems in psychosis is the failure of the ego's capacity to repress, so that the
psychotic is overwhelmed by, for example, incestuous wishes
of which the normal and neurotic, as a result of repression,
remain unaware. The second reason is that we have now
come to the realization that certain arrangements which were
formerly considered to be defensive are "adaptive." This idea,
first proposed by Hartmann, suggests that behavior may first
be adopted for its defensive value and yet may later become
so useful to the individual that it loses its primarily defensive
quality; it is then no longer pathological and may even become an activity which is pleasurable in its own right. We
think here of the analogy of the child who is forced to learn
to play the piano against his will, but who someday becomes
a skillful musician and begins to enjoy it and to want it for
himself. Reexamination of the case of Mrs. Bernard would be
also illustrative here. She becomes overly clean when she is
anxious. Those familiar with psychoanalytic theory will recog-

nize this as a *reaction-formation,* that is, a defense against the wish to soil by turning it into its opposite. However, in ordinary, everyday situations which are less burdened with anxiety, cleanliness and tidiness are necessary to efficient functioning. The business executive, teacher, secretary, scientist, among many others, would be unable to perform their daily work if they were not to keep documents, files, desk drawers, and the like in order. Thinking also involves a certain amount of orderliness if it is to be productive. Much of the world's work, on all levels, is carried on by persons who have turned their originally defensive reaction-formation against soiling and untidiness to adaptive advantage. Some persons acquire enjoyable hobbies such as painting and stamp collecting which are adaptive in the sense of no longer being direct expressions of the instinctual drive or the defense against it. In Mrs. Bernard's case, we may distinguish between her need to clean for defensive purposes and the adaptive nature of the housewife's tasks which include keeping the home pleasant.

Finally, and perhaps more important in theoretical order of precedence than the first two, is the reason that, by observing the defensive structure of the individual, we study, simultaneously, the characteristic way in which his ego operates. This tells us vastly more about him than the observation, in the early days of psychoanalysis, of the operation of the instinctual drives only. Today, both aspects of behavior—drive organization and ego functioning in terms of defense and adaptation—are of equal importance in the understanding of the individual. Looking at Mrs. Bernard once again with these factors in mind, we see that, in addition to *reaction-formation,* she uses another defense mechanism, *regression.* She states this in her opening remarks to the counselor, "I was so bothered and so completely at a loss as to what to do that I got down on the kitchen floor and gave it the scrubbing of its life." Implied here is that, under the impact of anxiety, regression takes place; this also implies that her less defensive level of psychosexual maturation is higher.° It seems almost self-evident that this much defensive behavior must employ large amounts of energy and this is precisely where the problem in defense lies—energy which would otherwise be available for growth and ego development is bound up in conflict, anxiety, and the defense against it.

Nevertheless, in degree of pathology, Mrs. Bernard is better off than is Mrs. Alfred, who has less adequate ego organization and therefore less defensive capacity. It is as though a nation must impoverish itself if it spends a disproportionate amount of its income on maintaining an army, but, if under attack, is in a better position than a nation which must yield to invasion because it cannot defend itself adequately. Mrs. Bernard, at great expense, defends herself against onslaughts of excessive anxiety; Mrs. Alfred does not have sufficient ego organization to muster defense.

Comparison of the states of anxiety and the defenses against it in both these cases brings us to another aspect of the differences between the well-organized and the inadequately developed ego in anxiety and defense. The better-developed ego is able to recognize anxiety as a signal for the institution of defenses which have become more or less automatic. To stay within the metaphor, there is a well-trained militia which goes into immediate mobilization when signaled that the enemy is approaching. The less-developed ego, as in the case of Mrs. Alfred, has no "militia," that is, no organized defensive system that can respond to "signal" anxiety. Therefore, Mrs. Alfred is vulnerable to even small amounts of anxiety which a stronger ego would be able to recognize, to tolerate or defend against.

° A thorough psychoanalytic exposition of Mrs. Bernard's neurosis would have to include consideration of other defense mechanisms, *isolation* and *undoing*, for example. For the purpose to be served here, we believe that this would be too lengthy and unrewarding a digression.

There are several types of anxiety which are reflective of a hierarchy of developmental levels, and these, too, are of importance in the understanding of anxiety and the defenses against it as the marital counselor encounters their manifestations. It has been speculated, and to some degree proved, that if the peaceful state in the womb is the prototype of absence of anxiety, then the birth process is the organism's first experience with prototypical anxiety. Greenacre, in an interesting study, correlates the extent of the anxiety with the extent of discomfort in birth. This varies in each individual and depends upon such factors as rapid versus prolonged labor, normal versus complicated delivery, lubricated versus "dry" birth canal, and similar variables which are relatively uncontrollable. Thus, each individual begins life with a different level of what Greenacre terms *basic anxiety*. It is apparent that, even in optimal circumstance, the human infant is predisposed to anxiety. Immediately after birth, this predisposition is increased because excessive stimuli, first experienced in the birth process, continue to impinge in ever-increasing amounts. There are also studies of infants which show that some degree of protection against excessive stimulation in the early months of life is provided by an inborn apparatus called the *stimulus barrier*. This exists in different individuals in varying degrees, and the matter is made even more complex by consideration that it is one of the maternal functions to provide the infant with protection against too much stimulation (such as light, noise, and the like) to supplement the operation of his own stimulus barrier. Thus, the most fortunate individual is one who has had full-term and uneventful intrauterine development, easy birth, possesses a relatively high stimulus barrier, *and* a mother who is so attuned that she herself constitutes a reserve stimulus barrier when she senses that the infant needs such reinforcement from her. If, even under such ideal circumstances, there remains a predisposition to anxiety, what about the overriding majority of situations which are short of this ideal? It has already been said that a degree of anxiety is a fact of life and that no one succeeds in living without some of it some of the time. In extreme cases, basic anxiety is so overwhelming that capacity to cope with it and to evolve defenses is impaired.

After the first few months of infancy, when the nurturing object is dimly perceived and the infant is at the level of need-gratification along the object-relations scale (see Chapter VI), another source of anxiety emerges. The dim awareness of the existence of the object coincides with an innate "knowledge" that survival is dependent upon her nurturing. Anxiety, at this stage of development, takes the form of fear of loss of the object, which coincides with fear of annihilation. At the next stage, when object relations proceed to the point of beginning object love, anxiety takes the form of fear of loss of love. It is at this stage that the child becomes "socializable" because he becomes willing to curb his instinctual demands for the sake of being loved. The demands of society, transmitted by the parent whose love is needed, acquire more importance than the demands of instinctual drive. Thus, the strictures of society (toilet-training and other behavioral requirements) may be imposed with success.

Such compliance on the child's part, however, does not assure relief from anxiety, but only changes the perception of the danger. Once love is more or less secured at the price of opposing anal wishes, anxiety shifts its "attention" to fantasied loss of parts of one's body. While this is a new and higher level of anxiety on the developmental scale, it cannot be described as a much more comfortable one so far as the individual who feels it is concerned. The child, uncertain about whether his excretions are parts of himself, gives them up reluctantly and often fearfully. When he reaches the phallic level, such fear extends to uncertainty about whether his genitalia are also detachable and expendable. Thus, he proceeds from one level of anxiety to the next, arriving at the level of castration anxiety with ego development which helps him experience himself as more of an integrated person than when he feared total annihilation. He is, however, only slightly more comfortable despite having succeeded in developing more ego organization and defenses along the way. In discussing superego development, we spoke of fear of the policeman, that is, fear of external punishment. It is at the phallic level, when castration anxiety reaches a height, that the fear of such punishment is greatest because the child, at the same time, has sexual and aggressive wishes and fantasies for which he expects to be punished.

The final phase in the scale of levels of anxiety coincides with the formation of the superego as an intact, internalized structure, and then one proceeds to the fear not of external punishment but of one's own conscience. This is when the ego must learn to modify behavior to conform with the demands of the superego as well as with the demands of reality. When the ego succeeds in this task, there are moments of relative freedom from anxiety (and, we might add, from guilt).*

What about those times when anxiety exists? There are many counseling situations when the patient presents himself

---

* The terms *fear* and *anxiety* are being used almost interchangeably here. Theoreticians make the distinction between fear of real danger and anxiety, which they define as fear of internal or fantasied danger. While such distinction is theoretically useful, we prefer to keep in the foreground that anxiety is an affect and, as such, feels as uncomfortable (or more so) as fear of real danger. For the purpose to be served here, it is considered that, making too great a distinction between fear and anxiety tempts the counselor to adopt the attitude that the problem is "only" anxiety. The patient is then placed in the difficult position of finding no sympathy with his discomfort, although it feels real enough to him. It seems preferable, therefore, to emphasize the affective quality of anxiety as similar to fear because we think that the patient will be better understood if the affective frame of reference is used.

as feeling anxious or is able to describe the conditions which make him anxious. More often, however, what the counselor encounters are the characteristic defenses against anxiety. The problem, then, is one of tracing back, that is, recognizing the defense and then looking behind it for the locus of anxiety. In the original establishment of the defense, it was the other way round—the anxiety, experienced as a signal by the ego, precipitated the establishment of defense and, each time similar circumstances reevoke anxiety, defense is once again mobilized. Mrs. David's unresolved incestuous wishes become reactivated and make her anxious each time Mr. David behaves in a fatherly manner toward her. The signal to reinforce the repression of these wishes operates rather smoothly for her, so that she experiences little anxiety and merely feels uninterested in sex. Mrs. Charles is somewhat less fortunate because she is on the verge of experiencing her castration anxiety too much of the time and is forced to insist upon the solution of having a baby lest the anxiety break through and become unbearable.

Mrs. Alfred's anxiety is of a different kind. We have already termed it *separation anxiety*. This is the characteristic anxiety in persons who have not successfully attained separation-individuation (see Chapter V) and who therefore fear that the absence of the symbiotic partner renders them incomplete because this partner, seen as part of the self, is the nurturing, need-gratifying, protective part and, as such, must be present all the time. This kind of anxiety is different from signal anxiety; it is overwhelming and subject to less effective defensive alleviation. Having fewer internal resources in the form of ego structure and defensive organization, Mrs. Alfred can only cling to her mother and maternal substitutes in great desperation. We ask in Chapter V why Mrs. Alfred has married and that question is also here pertinent because the Alfred case is an example of marriage which is employed as a defense. Mrs.

Alfred married because symbiotic wish for union with mother threatened identity. A heterosexual object, for her, is an opportunity to preserve identity by emphasis upon gender difference. However, the attempted solution does not succeed. Mrs. Alfred is on a seesaw. When her end of the seesaw is on the ground, she is with her mother. Out of fear of loss of identity and in the direction of separation-individuation, she moves toward her husband and finds herself in the air. She returns to mother again because the anxiety of separation is too great. She cannot really come to rest in either position. The entire marital situation is a maneuver in her endless search for surcease from anxiety.

Mrs. Bernard does not have to use the marriage as a defense. She has a well-enough structured ego to have developed more internalized methods. In psychoanalytic parlance, she has a symptom neurosis, more precisely, a compulsion neurosis. A symptom is a compromise, a peace treaty which tries to satisfy all belligerents. In Mrs. Bernard's case, her highest level of functioning approaches genitality. The weakness of this forward position causes it to yield at the slightest tinge of anxiety. The mechanism of defense called *regression* sends her back to the anal level in the hope of avoiding anxiety. In this psychosexual position, the instinctual wish—to soil—becomes prominent and causes further anxiety. Another defense, *reaction-formation,* has to be summoned to oppose this wish. Finally, despite the regression, the instinctual demand at the higher level threatens to emerge and thus joins forces with the anal wish, so that the compulsion to clean is the only final solution to otherwise unbearable anxiety. When Mrs. Bernard says, "I *have to* scrub the floor," she is conveying that she is compelled and, to the counselor who understands anxiety and defense, that there is really no choice. It has already been observed that considerable ego organization is involved but also that much psychic energy is expended in such elaborate defensive arrangement. Another rather important aspect of Mrs. Bernard's defensive structure is that its total mode of operation tends to protect her object relations. This is described in Chapter IV where we state that she does not attack her husband, she attacks the floor. While the aggression is apparent, its deflection is noteworthy. For the counselor, this is a clear indication that the marriage is not at the core of Mrs. Bernard's problem and that she is more readily available for individual therapy than is the person who begins his search for treatment by projecting upon the marriage. Mrs. Bernard says, "*I* get upset when . . ." not "*He* makes me. . . ."

The same cannot be said of Mr. Bernard. We have here the very interesting counseling problem of one spouse who is able to accept and acknowledge an internalized problem which needs treatment and the other whose view of the problem does involve the marriage. None of our other cases illustrates quite so sharply the dilemma posed by the question of whether it is the individual or the marriage that should be the focus of treatment. How shall the counselor begin treatment when one of the partners is aware that she has individual problems and the other regards the marriage as the problem? When Mrs. Bernard behaves in a way that makes Mr. Bernard feel uncomfortable, his anxiety takes the form of fear that he is losing the needed closeness with the object; if he attempts to decrease the distance between them at such moments in the attempt to allay his separation anxiety, he encounters another source of anxiety in the form of becoming too much like her and therefore losing gender identity. Out of all this, the tip of the iceberg which he presents to the counselor is his anger about his wife's behavior. If the counselor follows the fundamental therapeutic rule—begin where the patient is—he has, in marital counseling, not one but two different individuals who are at different initial vantage points in their views of the problem. The question of where to begin, therefore, resolves itself with understanding the individual psychology of each spouse. One begins with each separately and differently. The versatility of the human being in arranging defenses is almost infinite. Although this is favorable because it means that individuals, under the stress of anxiety, have many resources to draw from, it makes it understandably difficult for the counselor to recognize defenses. This is particularly true because the counselor is always confronted with patients who employ not a single defense but combinations of defenses. Even more complex arrangements involve the employment of one instinctual drive against another in the service of defense. While complex, however, it is essential that the marriage counselor familiarize himself with these. One of the most common forms of one instinctual drive against another in marriage is the employment of heterosexuality against homosexuality. In psychoanalytic language, this is often described as a "flight forward," that is, the individual engages in a mode of behavior which, in the maturational and developmental scale, is ahead of his actual level of fixation. The anxiety aroused by homosexual wishes is so great that a flight into heterosexuality takes place. Mrs. Alfred's reason for marrying may be understood, in part, this way. An aspect of Mr. Bernard's problem has already been touched upon in this regard, but may be explained more thoroughly here. He becomes so disturbed about his wife's behavior not only because it leaves him out but because he feels an unconscious identification with her femininity which he then has to ward off by speaking unpleasantly to her. Much quarreling and unpleasantness between marital partners may be understood as employing sadistic remarks or action to defend against "sympathizing" too much. Such sympathy may be threatening because of the fear of symbiotic merger; because of the danger of overidentification which brings on fear of homosexuality, and, as in the case of Mrs. David, because of fear of heterosexual incestuous wishes. When quarreling is recognized as a sign of something defensive, the counselor is in a good position to deal with it by trying to understand its place and purpose in the individual's defensive structure. The counselor's diagnostic "ego" learns to recognize quarreling as a "signal."

When marriage is undertaken as a defense against latent homosexual wishes and against the concomitant anxiety that these would arouse, the "security" of marriage is called upon to serve as affirmation of heterosexuality. Some of the consequent complications in marriage when it is employed as such a solution have already been touched upon. Its hampering effect upon the developmental aspect of marriage may be emphasized here. When marriage is used for such defensive purposes, a heavy burden is placed upon it to prove heterosexuality in the face of constantly reemerging homosexual wishes. The more growth-promoting possibilities within marriage are sacrificed for the sake of the defense. A prime example of this is the failure to use marriage for the building of object relations and for the final resolution of the oedipal ties.

Mr. Irving has always had many men friends and continued these friendships after marriage. He looks forward to rigidly fixed evenings and sometimes weekends "with the boys." While it is to be expected that friendships that are meaningful will remain after marriage, it is also to be expected that their quality and intensity will change. Such qualitative and quantitative alteration is necessary if the developmental features in the marital relationship are to be realized because, energy devoted to continuing relationships outside marriage to the same degree as before is thereby unavailable for the building of new object relations within the marriage (see Chapter X).

The experienced counselor is familiar with complaints which are expressed in the form of how many evenings the spouse spends out with the "boys" or "girls." Some of the diagnostic questions which the counselor may bear in mind concern not *how many* evenings but how rigidly must they be maintained without consideration for what is going on in the home; what internal needs do they serve; is the primary motive the athletic activity or entertainment or is it excessive need for companions of the same sex? By searching in this manner it may be determined whether marriage is used primarily for defense against homosexuality that would threaten to go beyond the evenings out. If this is so, treatment proceeds to enable the patient to understand his needs and wishes and to progress in his psychological development. Superficial arrangements such as how many nights to spend at home, whether responsibility to wife and children take precedence over nights out, and the like are of no avail. Therapy in depth, however, provides excellent prognosis in many instances.

Anxiety, guilt, and depression are the most unpleasant affective states the human being can experience. It is understandable, therefore, that marriage as well as divorce are two of many devices the individual would tend to employ in the attempt to rid himself of these extremely uncomfortable feelings. The case material presented thus far illustrates how marriage is sometimes sought as a solution to intolerable anxiety, that is, as a defense. We iterate some of these would-be solutions here. Mrs. Alfred seeks to escape annihilation, loss of identity, separation anxiety, and probably depression as well. Mr. Bernard also seeks, in marriage, to avoid separation anxiety only to find himself confronted with a deeper anxiety concerning gender identity and homosexuality. Mrs. Charles looks for solution of penis envy and castration anxiety in marriage and motherhood. Mr. and Mrs. Edward use marriage to prevent separation anxiety. Mr. Frank wishes for the "good" object because aggression toward the "bad" object would bring on unbearable anxiety. Mrs. George and Mr. Harold married in the unconscious hope that the partner would constitute an adequate superego that is missing in their internal structures. We do not mean to convey that these were the sole motivations for these marriages but only to convey the defensive aspect of complex sets of motivations.

While marriage that is entered into for defensive purposes nevertheless usually contains, as we have maintained, developmental potential which may be released with skillful counseling, divorce must be regarded somewhat differently. Probably one of the most difficult and also most essential diagnostic challenges is the determination of whether divorce is a projected solution which consists primarily of defense and escape or whether the only growth-promoting opportunity lies in the direction of terminating the marriage. This statement implies that divorce may be growth-promoting only when it is used to dissolve a marriage which is growth-inhibiting. Once again, as in many aspects of adult life which we have discussed here, this point of view imposes a consideration of divorce different from the moral, legal, or religious—although moral, legal, and religious thought often coincide without contradiction with the views proposed here. Divorce may be regarded as a last rather than a first resort and can only be determined to be validly employed after the growth potential in the marriage has been fully explored. Divorce undertaken hastily, aggressively, punitively, defensively is familiar enough, as is remarriage wherein the same problems as in the previous marriage crop up. Probably no other single area of marital counseling involves as much skill and suspension of judgment on the part of the counselor as the exploration with the patient of whether divorce is indeed the solution to the problem. In the case of Mr. Alfred, after such exploration, he decided to remain with his wife despite the glaring problems she presents. The patient's own decision regarding divorce is central, because competent counseling *in itself* promotes growth, one feature of which is the patient's autonomy in matters which affect his life. The counselor, therefore, never "recommends" divorce, but brings the patient to understand his unconscious need for the spouse, helps him release his growth potential where it is blocked, and then leaves him free to make his own decision. Divorce undertaken in the service of defense (against fear of closeness or fear of sex, for example) is usually not considered in the light of self-understanding and is therefore likely to fail to provide new opportunities for growth and self-fulfillment. The decision should be made at leisure and only after full exploration of the problems in the marriage. By this means, more marriages would endure and the sometimes severe problems in them might even be resolved.

Mr. Frank tends to discard the "bad" object in his unending but futile search for the "good" one. How such a marriage, without the benefit of counseling, can easily terminate in divorce is apparent. Almost all the cases already described might have gone on to divorce at critical moments in the marriage. Those in which the object relations are less fully developed are the most "divorceable" because absence of object constancy leads toward interchangeability of the object.

Mr. and Mrs. James's problems were best resolved by divorce. Married for seventeen years, with three children, sixteen, thirteen, and eleven years of age, they tended to ignore their difficulties and pretend that all was well. Mr. James had a small retail business which he ran by himself and which kept him away from home because of the long hours he believed he had to work. It is always difficult, in such situations, to assess the reality of the husband's need to be away and the counselor is wise not to initiate questions about this too early in treatment lest he reinforce the firm insistence that this is indeed a reality. Later, when the transference is well-established and the wish to work with the counselor is unconsciously as well as consciously earnest, the patient himself usually begins to look at the deployment of his time away from home by raising his own questions about the real necessity versus the avoidance of problems within the home. Such was the case with Mr. James who, only after a long period of counseling, found the courage to look more closely at what was going on at home. The oldest girl's detainment by the juvenile court forced him to bring his concern about his children to consideration with the counselor. Gradually, because such matters are so difficult for a man like Mr. James to face, the counselor helped him see that his children were neglected. While Mr. James's income was sufficient to provide the necessities of life, it was not much more than that. Nevertheless, we do not mean neglect in the form of material deprivation, but are referring to psychological neglect. The children were left on their own too much of the time even though Mrs. James was not working and was assumed to be mother and housewife. They were not wakened to go to school, not given regular meals, nor prevented from coming and going as they pleased, even at night. The oldest daughter was picked up for truancy, although it might be said here that she was not really a deliberate truant, rather that habits of regularity, work, and responsibility had never been taught. Mr. James's concern about the outcome of the juvenile court hearing brought him for counseling. Mrs. James was also seen, by another counselor in the same clinic. This separation proved invaluable later for many reasons; the most important was that the marriage proceeded ultimately to divorce and the two counselors were available separately to both partners. This arrangement is far more advantageous for transference and countertransference than one where one counselor finds himself in the middle of a deteriorating marriage.

Although Mrs. James's counselor diagnosed rather quickly that Mrs. James did not have sufficient ego strength to be an adequate mother, we wish to make it clear that it is often not necessary for such a partner to be seen for diagnostic purposes; Mr. James's counselor would, in time, have been able to learn much about Mrs. James indirectly. However, since Mrs. James was seen, the diagnostic information was useful. It was also revealing to know that she came for counseling more out of fear of the court than because of inner motivation. (In this respect, the level of superego development which involves fear of the "policeman" instead of regulation by one's own inner values is of interest.) It became clearer in the course of counseling both partners that this was one of those all too frequent situations in which a rather disturbed and unable-to-function woman is protected for many years within a marital situation which obviates earning a living. Although the home was untidy and showed many other signs of nonfunctioning, Mr. James had blinded himself to this for years. The defense mechanism of denial was in operation, and the counselor knew that when such a defense is employed it is because the patient cannot bear to face the facts. Very gradually, then, the counselor tried to understand Mr. James and to help Mr. James understand himself. He was found to be a hard-working man who demanded very little and who needed the illusion of a smoothly knit family so badly that he could not afford, psychologically, to see that the reality was otherwise. He had come from a broken home and was determined that his marital home would be a good one. He did not, however, know how to choose a wife wisely for this purpose. As we have said about all marriage in Western culture, the choices are dictated by unconscious factors. Unconsciously, Mr. James needed someone on the need-gratification level (Chapter VI) and chose a woman for whom he could do what he needed himself. This is not an unusual form of reversal. Early in the marriage, thus functioning in accordance with his own need in reverse form, he did much of the housework, cooking, and even "mothering" of the babies. Only years later was it possible to understand that this saved the children from no mothering at all, but at much psychological expense to all. In a manner that was not seen as related at the time, Mr. James's interest in his business increased as the children began to grow out of babyhood. He then regarded himself as the breadwinner and found some growth-promoting features in this, particularly with regard to his masculine self-image. Unfortunately, this development could occur only by his failing to notice the daily indications of a nonfunctioning wife and mother and neglect of the children.*

* Since this is a book on marriage and not specifically on child care, we are not detailing at length the factors in the mother-child relationship that necessitate her maternal availability at *all* phases of development. We have said much about this aspect of mothering as it pertains to the first few years of life and have implied that phase-appropriate mothering is a necessity until the child becomes an adult. Counselors are, these days, encountering more and more children, adolescents, and adults who were neglected children in the sense that we are using the word here. We feel therefore that a brief explanation that the most favorable growth situation for the child is the presence of two functioning parents in the home is in order. We cannot here go into the many problems that ensue when the father is absent, although one aspect has been discussed—the establishment of gender identity and the resolution of the oedipus complex are impaired. When the mother or a suitable substitute is absent or, as in the case of Mrs. James, is nonfunctioning, the children are required to perform the task of "bringing themselves up." With no experience in such matters and with phase-specific needs which conflict with such too-early self-sufficiency, success is rare. One of the most dramatic and socially undesirable consequences of this type of neglect is delinquency, which arises out of simply not knowing what to do, how to conduct oneself, looking to similarly inexperienced peers for what is lacking in the home. The psychologically undesirable consequences are absence of an adequate figure for identification, absence of feeling loved, absence of opportunity for internalization, and the formation of an adequate superego.

As the case unfolded, it also became evident that Mrs. James's problems were not only her psychological nonfunctioning as a mother; her physical absence, often when she should have been at home with the children; but also her unconscious need to use the children for purposes destructive to them. She was psychologically unable to maintain the important and necessary line of demarcation between the generations, so that she exposed the children to her bathing and toileting functions (see the discussion of stimulus barrier, page 107) and to sex talk that was more confusing and overstimulating than enlightening. She often took one or another of them into bed with her because of her need for closeness, but in disregard for their need for separation-individuation and absence of sexual stimulation. Also, she involved them in marital quarreling, complaining to them about their father as a husband and trying to get them to take sides with her against him. Mrs. James's counselor concluded, after eight months of treatment, that Mrs. James's ego was so impaired and her motivation for change so limited, that not much more than minimally supportive work could be done with her. Mr. James, in his counseling sessions, not only found growth potential within himself but was able, out of this, to acquire more capacity to endure separation-individuation, a higher level of object relations which involved more concern for his children, and, on the practical level, a wish to provide a more growth-promoting home for them. He concluded, after· one and one-half years of intensive counseling, that a divorce was necessary as the best means of enabling him to establish a new home. This was without haste to remarry, but only to give himself and his children a chance to grow. He decided to provide adequately for Mrs. James because she would never be able to support herself, and let the question of remarriage await its own phase-specific moment.

CHAPTER IX

Sex in Marriage

PSYCHOTHERAPISTS, counselors, and even physicians conducting medical examination used to be taught to ask of a person seeking psychological or medical treatment, "Is your sex life satisfactory?" It was thought that the answer to this question would provide clues about the individual's general psychological and physical well-being. This idea was based upon an early and now superseded theory that "dammed-up" sexual energy created a "toxic" state that made the individual prone to neurosis and often led to physical symptoms as well. Even these days, in common parlance, an irritable or otherwise unpleasant person is characterized as "frustrated," with emphasis upon the implication that the absence of satisfactory sexual outlet accounts for the difficulty.

Most persons are loath to reveal their sex practices and particularly their sex problems and inadequacies. Generally, they come for counseling presenting problems which, in their minds, are focused around other aspects of the marital relationship; sexual aspects come into the discussion only as treatment progresses and transference is established. Even when it happens, as it sometimes does, that a couple wishes to begin treatment around sex problems, it is more profound to regard the sex problem as symptomatic of other problems in their personalities. For diagnostic purposes, the counselor should also realize that, if the patient talks too openly too soon about sexual matters, this may signify faulty ego development. While such is not always the case, the counselor is wise to be wary about priding himself in having established good rapport before investigating whether the too easy revelation of intimate facts is indicative of weak defenses and poor object relations. The patient who "pours out" before transference is established may be "relating" too quickly because he is like the person who is hungry and does not care who brings the food or the person who is sexually promiscuous because his level of object relations renders him incapable of feeling that anyone in particular matters more than anyone else. As is true of many aspects of psychoanalytic psychology, both extremes are matters for diagnostic concern—the person who talks too freely may be suffering from severe ego pathology, the one who defends so heavily that he can never tell the counselor about intimate matters may have too great a stake in maintaining his defenses.

It is indicated in earlier chapters that sexual behavior may encompass purposes other than fulfillment of genital needs and discharge of genital tension. We may use the case of Mrs. Charles to illustrate here how futile it would be to discuss with her, too early in treatment, the matter of how satisfactory her sex life feels to her. Driven as she is by the urgency to conceive a child in order to lessen anxiety about unconsciously fantasied physical deficiency, it can hardly be expected that she would lend herself to leisurely consideration of the quality of the sexual relationship. Her primary conscious purpose is to engage in sexual relations without contraceptives, regardless of other criteria of satisfaction. Therefore, if she were to be asked the initial question about satisfaction, the question would elicit a positive or negative response within a frame of reference which differs from that of the questioner; her answer, then, would tend to be misleading rather than enlightening. More meaningful information is gathered by refraining from asking essentially unanswerable questions too soon. This does not mean that such a question is not sometimes useful for diagnostic purposes and for correlating initial response with later material, as long as the counselor keeps in mind this purpose and does not take the conscious answer too much at face value. In the case of Mrs. Charles, the counselor must realize that, regardless of how she answers, the genital aspects of sexual relations are diminished and are replaced by the goal of reduction of anxiety via acquisition of a phallus-baby.

Similar deflection of genital goal is discernible, after some scrutiny, in our other cases. Mr. Alfred told the counselor that sexual relations have been given up almost entirely. Where orality dominates to the extent found in Mrs. Alfred, genitality is not as important as is oral gratification. Since Mr. Alfred joins her in this stage of psychosexuality, they find less obvious means to attain oral pleasure, as in eating, and they use the marital intimacy for oral forms of discharge as well.

While Mrs. Alfred's symbiotic needs have also been stressed, in her case the oral fixation determines the nature of her sexual behavior. When oral fixation is not so pronounced, while symbiotic need persists, the sexual behavior takes a somewhat different form. Mr. and Mrs. Edward, who need to be "close" and in a constant state of "togetherness," are not so much interested in oral forms of sex; the dominant goal of their sexual activity is that they gratify the need for closeness and body contact. This kind of "sexual" relatedness is even more dramatically evident to the counselor who treats persons who seek body closeness regardless of the specific relationship with the partner: persons of both sexes who use the first date for such gratification, before they get to know the partner; promiscuous persons; the homosexual, often mistakenly described as "bisexual," who is really neither homosexual nor heterosexual but is more like the person whose hunger can be satisfied by any "server"—waiter or waitress.

It is not intended to imply that any one of the varied forms of sexual behavior is in and of itself pathological or, as sometimes has been termed with all too judgmental a connotation, "infantile." For example, babies do need to be held, and a residue of this "skin hunger" persists throughout life. Normal sexual relations reproduce the infant's pleasurable experiences with bodily contact and is one of the gratifications toward the more intense pleasure of genital discharge; in other words, it is part of the forepleasure. For Mr. and Mrs. Edward, however, it has more of the quality of an endpleasure because of the dominance of symbiotic over genital need. We have begun, in this way, to describe how sex, which is a most important aspect of the marital relationship, is best understood by the counselor as an integral part of his understanding of the maturational and developmental features which lead the individual in the direction of sexual maturity.

In Chapter IV, it is shown that the child's maturation encompasses pregenital levels of sexuality before the genital level is reached. While the genital personality has been characterized as tender, loving, tolerant, considerate, giving, patient, and functioning on the level of object constancy which involves a continuing relationship with one person, this is purely descriptive and tells us little about the internal aspects of genitality and about how the individual arrives at this level of psychosexual maturation.

It is probably most realistic to regard genitality as the psychosexual goal toward which the fortunately endowed individual in favorable life circumstances develops. He begins in the oral phase and matures through the several psychosexual phases, simultaneously undergoing personality structuralization, accomplishing separation-individuation, differentiating self representations from object representations to acquire identity and object relations, and perfecting ego and superego functions. By the time he reaches the phallic-oedipal phase, if development and maturation have proceeded successfully, he is as well-equipped as is possible for his encounter with the oedipal task. This, as indicated, requires all the resources at his command. When the oedipal child makes his bow to reality and begins to relinquish his oedipal wish, substituting identification with the parent of the same sex for rivalry with him, he enters the period of latency. These few quiescent years provide opportunity for ego building, only to yield at puberty to a reemergence of large quantities of libidinous and aggressive energy and to a second round in the struggle with the oedipal wish. This time, the task is paradoxically more difficult but, at the same time, more readily accomplished —more difficult because physical maturation makes the gratification of sexual desire realistically possible; more favorable to resolution because, if the first round is reasonably successful, if ego development is favorable, and if the parents remain benign and uninvolved in the many irritating and provocative features of the adolescent's overt behavior, the psychological foundation for success is at hand. Returning to the analogy of the brick wall, it may be said here again that if the bottom rows are evenly and securely laid, the upper rows rest more firmly upon them. This is not to say that the developmental task of adolescence is at all an easy one or that it is quickly accomplished; it merely describes the optimal conditions for success.

Marriage, we maintain, offers a third and final opportunity for the resolution of residual oedipal wishes and the overcoming of the incest taboo. How successfully this is mastered depends largely upon the strengths of the instinctual drives and the degree of neutralization and of ego development; if the wish remains overpowering, then it is all the more difficult for the individual to distinguish past wish from present reality and to abandon childhood desire in favor of sanctioned sexual relations with the real partner who is a contemporary. This is the problem with Mrs. David, who, driven by the unattenuated force of her childhood love for her father, unconsciously mistakes husband for father and then founders on the incest taboo which rightfully belonged to the past.

Thus far, our examples describe the normal developmental opportunity within marriage for the final relinquishment of oedipal wish and oedipal object. What of the myriad sex problems, which the marriage counselor encounters, that stem from less than the ideal life situations sketched? We now turn our attention to these.

Persons who respond in the affirmative to the question "Is your sex life satisfactory?" are, like Mrs. Charles, telling the truth as they see it. That the individual who is having the experience and reports it to the counselor is unable to report accurately in some instances is explained by several factors, now quite familiar to the reader: 1) the unconscious, 2) psychosexual level on which the pleasure is attained, 3) level of object relations, 4) defensive structure, and 5) intactness of ego functions.*

We know that because of the unconscious an individual may have an experience or perform an act without being aware of his motivations. Now, a further question may arise: What difference does an awareness of motivation make as long as the experience is satisfactory? The only answer possible in a study of marital counseling is that those couples whose sexual relationship is as satisfactory as they say are not

---

* Kinsey's extensive studies served a valuable purpose in bringing sex knowledge as a reality of life to the attention of scientists. A major flaw in his methodology, however, is his failure to take the above factors into account. He disregards the unconscious, naïvely believing that the statements made to his interviewers by sincerely motivated subjects were factual. He considers, also, that the physical experience of orgasm can be counted as a statistical unit without regard for the essential factors which determine the nature and quality of the event. For a more complete critique of Kinsey's work, see R. P. Knight, "Psychiatric Issues in the Kinsey Report on Males," in Knight, ed., *Psychoanalytic Psychiatry and Psychology*.

likely to present themselves for counseling. Candidates for counseling do employ projection and displacement to a large degree. Therefore, when the report is disharmony in other aspects of the relationship and yet satisfaction in sex, the counselor should be alerted to a probable imbalance somewhere. A fairly common psychological arrangement in which apparently adequate sexual functioning operates as a defense is *layering*. By this is meant that the uppermost and visible layer may be one of satisfaction; the layer beneath this would be impotence or frigidity, covered over by the apparent good functioning; beneath that lies fixation in pregenital and pre-oedipal levels of which the impotence or frigidity is symptomatic. In such manner, pseudosexual adequacy is attained by considerable expenditure of psychic energy, for, as we explained in Chapter VIII, it takes energy to construct a symptom and then to cover it over with another layer of defense. Mr. Charles's problem illustrates this type of *layering*.

Mr. and Mrs. Charles, in the initial stages of counseling, were unwilling to go into their sex problem. This was to be expected, since their starting point was baby now versus baby later. As the transference developed, the counselor learned more about the sexual aspects of the marital relationship. Mr. Charles, proud of his intellect, was similarly proud of his penis and its perfect functioning. He was not at all aware of how unconscious fears of damage to it influenced his behavior. Such defenses are difficult to work through. Haste on the counselor's part is likely to threaten and therefore to increase Mr. Charles's insistence that everything is perfect. Excessive expenditure of energy in the defensive process is pertinent here. Adequate functioning in a man who is more secure in his masculinity would be more relaxed and effortless. That Mr. Charles has to work so hard at it alerts the counselor to the defensive aspects. It is sometimes said in therapy that things have to get worse before they get better. For Mr.

Charles, this means that, in long term treatment, he would probably develop a temporary partial impotence. While this appears to be an unfavorable turn in the treatment, actually it is quite favorable because it would mean that the ego-syntonic functioning has been replaced by an ego-dystonic symptom, that the defense is less operative, and that treatment can proceed toward real potency rather than defensively motivated potency. These are the possibilities in optimal treatment of the patient who wishes to undertake counseling with a psychoanalytically trained therapist.

Mrs. Charles's sex problem revolves around her intense envy of the male organ and her own sense of "organ inferiority." In intercourse, such feelings prevent her from appreciating her own sexual apparatus and the pleasure that the sex act can give her. Therefore, she is usually unable to attain orgasm, taking her failure in conjunction with her husband's apparently excellent functioning as reason to reinforce her envy and to wish for a baby as compensation. The further treatment of Mrs. Charles almost suggests itself. She needs help to become conscious of her wishes and fantasies and to begin to value her femininity. If this is successful, she will inevitably be a better mother than she would be if she were to have a baby to satisfy unconscious wishes unrelated to what a baby really is.

Detection of sex problems which are relatively unknown to the patient and barely visible to the counselor, except by inference, calls for diagnostic skill. We propose a list of the more important diagnostic questions which should arise in the counselor's mind when evaluating the nature of the problem. These are not necessarily intended as questions to be asked directly of the patient.

1. Is the experience satisfactory to both or to only one of the partners?

2. What are the pregenital practices in the foreplay?

3. Do these practices contribute to or overshadow the genital act?

4. Where does the dominant pleasure lie? In foreplay; in orgasm? In being together? In being with one particular person?

5. Is the quality of the relatedness tender, cruel, masochistic, indifferent?

6. How frequently does the couple engage in intercourse?

7. Is the act and its frequency consistent with other aspects of their relationship?

8. What do the details of the sex act reveal about the dominant psychosexual level?

9. Is sex used as a defense? If so, against what? Aggression? Loneliness? Homosexuality? Negation of problems?

10. What are the fantasies, if any, during the sex act? These may reveal much about the continued relationship to past objects.

Diagnostic questions such as these suggest a revision of the question, "Is your sex life satisfactory?" to "What is being satisfied?" and clearly implies that absence of satisfaction is usually only conscious and manifest. Again, the tip of the iceberg is the least of the matter and unconscious gratifications, even in experiences which appear manifestly as suffering, exist. The question "What is being satisfied?" is usually best kept in the mind of the counselor because the patient, particularly in the beginning, cannot respond with what, by definition, he does not know, that is, what is in his unconscious. However, when there are complaints of absence of gratification or even in the extreme of physical and psychic pain, the counselor should know as a theoretical guide that some gratification lies hidden.

Sexual symptoms per se are broadly described under the over-all headings of *impotence* and *frigidity*. These cover a wide range and may be either total or, more often, partial. A man may be impotent all of the time and in all situations; he may be impotent with one woman and potent with another; he may be potent only in homosexual encounters, but heterosexually impotent; he may have erectile capability for masturbatory purposes only, with or without fantasies and with or without perverse acts and stimulations such as exhibitionism, voyeurism, sadism, fetishism, or the like; he may be capable of erection only by means of such perverse acts as prelude to intercourse; he may be erectile only when consummation is not required of him; he may suffer from retarded ejaculation or from the most common of all potency problems in marriage, premature ejaculation. In addition, the quality of the orgasm, when there is one, should be carefully investigated in an evaluation of potency. Also to be considered by the counselor is that, when the patient speaks of impotence, he is likely to have in mind something which may differ from what the counselor thinks it means. If it is the wife who complains about the husband's impotence, what *she* means by this may have still another meaning. For example, if she is hostile, she may merely wish to be deprecatory; if she is frigid, she may speak of premature ejaculation when, in fact, the husband's potency may be quite adequate even though "premature" for her.

Premature ejaculation itself may range over a wide area, from *ejaculatio ante portem,* which makes penetration impossible, to ejaculation immediately upon intromission or so shortly thereafter as to be inadequate for pleasure of either partner. At the other extreme, delayed ejaculation or none is encountered in some men. The causes usually are not physical, are unconscious, and may only be understood on the basis of the individual's psychological makeup. A few generalities are suggested here as guides: Much male impotence has been generally understood to involve fear of castration and fear of the vagina; the impatient quality in premature ejaculation adds a dimension which suggests that the aspect of inability to wait stems from the early months of life and may have more to do with the oral phase than was heretofore considered. Similarly, delayed ejaculation may have to do with fear of loss of parts of one's body, which stems from the anal-phallic phase and contains elements of inability to give; it may also, however, involve inability to terminate the contact by taking the penis away. The diagnostic relevance of the quality of the orgasm is mentioned as a consideration in the investigation of a man's potency. This may range from intense pleasure to ejaculation without orgasm and includes many shadings between these. The fact that the quality of the orgasm can vary provides one explanation for the strange phenomenon whereby satisfaction is reported when full orgastic potency is not attained. A man may believe that his sexual experience is satisfactory simply because he has never known full orgasm. It is particularly important for the counselor to be alert to such lesser goals in men with masochistic tendencies—in the kind of person who is always ready to settle for too little in life.

Continuation of adolescent masturbation into adult life when heterosexual intercourse is available must also be regarded as a sexual problem. If masturbation is going on, eliciting the fantasies is of importance similar to that described in relation to intercourse fantasies.

Frigidity is the broad heading which encompasses a variety of female sexual problems. These range from total disinterest and even abhorrence of intercourse, incapacity to respond to sexual stimulation, through various forms of partial frigidity. Partial frigidity would include some pleasure in intercourse, but not of orgastic intensity, capacity for clitoral but not vaginal orgasm, and the ability to respond to pregenital forms of stimulation in preference to heterosexual intercourse. As in the case of the man, the woman, too, may retain an

interest in masturbation as the preferred form of sexual gratification; she may long for homosexual contact; she may use
heterosexual contact as a defense against homosexual tendencies.

The Masters and Johnson study has been particularly valuable in adding to our knowledge of the complex structure of
the female physical and psychological sexual apparatus. Their
work challenges one of the long-held psychoanalytic beliefs
about female sexual functioning, the so-called *transfer theory*.
Transfer theory maintains that the psychosexual maturation
of the boy and the girl are the same up to and including the
phallic phase, and, at this phase, the clitoris represents a
phallus and constitutes the locus of erogenous pleasure analogous to the penis. It was thought that only when the genital
phase is reached does the girl "transfer" orgastic potential
from clitoris to vagina which thereafter remains the female
organ of adult sexuality. Masters and Johnson found that the
normal female orgasm is neither solely clitoral nor solely
vaginal, but that the totality of the female sexual apparatus is
involved. Here again, the inquiry, for the marital counselor,
would lead in the direction of the quality of the orgasm and,
in this regard, the same questions apply as in the case of the
male. Because of the greater feminine proclivity for masoch-
ism, it is even more important to explore whether the patient is
settling for too little pleasure.

We are somewhat less impressed with the attempt by Masters and Johnson to foster sexual adjustment in couples who
present problems of sexual incompatibility. While there is no
doubt that the reports of success are accurate, it seems that the
adjustments attained are mechanical rather than developmental in the sense that we use developmental concepts here. In
other words, the methods in themselves do not seem to contain
opportunity for psychological growth into a higher stage of
development. The thesis of developmental potential in mar-

riage would preclude total reliance upon adjustment and accommodation which, although more rapidly attained, are less likely to endure. A follow-up study of the Masters and Johnson couples after a period of years would determine whether their procedures lead to permanent adjustment of the sex problem. The study should include investigation of whether and how psychological growth has taken place. It is possible, but remains to be proved, that psychological gain from overcoming sexual incompatibility leads to further development within marriage.

Another challenge to the transfer theory comes from psychoanalysts themselves, from the observation that the infant girl can experience vaginal sensation long before the phallic and genital phases are reached. Consideration of frigidity raises collateral questions within psychoanalytic theory with regard to female sexuality. The psychoanalytic theory of neurosis holds that, since neurosis is based in the failure of the resolution of the oedipus complex, frigidity in the neurotic woman is the logical consequence of sexual inhibition because of the incest taboo or of regression to earlier psychosexual levels. Sexuality is repressed because it has the quality of a forbidden wish. As psychoanalysts began to treat more and more women in the borderline and psychotic diagnostic categories, they found that, whereas the neurotic woman is likely to suffer from varying degrees of frigidity, the more disturbed woman is sometimes more capable of full vaginal orgasm than is her relatively healthier neurotic sister. This apparent contradiction, however, does not vitiate the psychoanalytic theory of neurosis if we apply what has been discussed in earlier chapters, particularly in Chapter VI. The neurotic woman, having reached the oedipal phase, is very much involved with her oedipal objects and has sufficient ego organization to have instituted defenses against her oedipal-sexual wishes. The more disturbed woman, likely to be functioning on the level of need-gratification, is less "encumbered" by object relations and can sometimes achieve orgasm more readily, but without object constancy, with less relatedness to the partner, and often promiscuously.

According to the transfer theory today, the incapacity for vaginal orgasm in the neurotic woman may be regarded not as failure to shift from clitoris to vagina in passing from the phallic to the genital phase but rather as a partial frigidity. The reasons for such difficulty require further study and conceptualization, including consideration of how the mental representation of the sexual apparatus is established.

Some problems in sexual functioning are based in failure to have mastered the separation-individuation crisis and are seen in individuals who are not able to regard the other person as distinct and separate and who do not have an identity of their own. We have already indicated that the moment of orgasm in normal sexual intercourse tends to replicate symbiotic reunion. Such temporary regression is tolerable in the ego that has attained a well-established sense of identity via individuation and can control the regression by reversing its direction and thus regaining identity when the sex act is over. In persons whose separateness is less firmly established, there may be fear of merger because the ego is less certain of its ability to restore identity. This phenomenon accounts for some types of frigidity and impotence in persons who would have greater orgastic capacity if there were less fear of symbiotic merger and therefore less need to guard against it by avoiding orgasm.

We have not detailed all of the sexual aberrations and perversions because that is not our purpose here. It may suffice to state that each can be traced diagnostically to a given stage of psychosexual maturation and ego development. The counselor is more concerned with establishing the level at which the patient is functioning than with the act per se. Specific information permits an approach, at least tentatively, to conclusions regarding level of functioning. A few simple examples are: If the end pleasure involves principally oral acts, then the counselor knows that there is oral fixation or regression; if the pleasure lies in infliction of pain or desire for suffering, then anality is involved; if there is great emphasis upon showing and looking, phallic exhibitionism is likely to be a factor; if there is promiscuity, there may be problems in object relations; if the purpose is primarily to be close to someone, symbiotic wishes may be involved. Consideration should also be given to behavior which is not overtly sexual but which gratifies pregenital sexual needs indirectly. The Bernard case illustrates this. Mrs. Bernard is so involved with the cleanliness of the floor because of her anal wishes; Mr. Bernard's caustic remarks also derive in part from anality. Such partial discharge of sexual energy drains away from the sexual act. Couples who quarrel excessively sometimes reach a climax of rage which contains an orgastic quality.

In no other aspect of married life are the interrelated problems of the spouses likely to be so clearly manifest as in their sexual relationship. Mr. and Mrs. Kenneth have been married for one and one-half years and have not yet consummated their marriage because Mr. Kenneth is impotent for purposes of sexual intercourse. Mrs. Kenneth complains bitterly about this and, on the face of it, feels quite justified both in her complaints and in her insistence that only Mr. Kenneth has a problem. It is obvious that he has. Less obvious, however, is that Mrs. Kenneth has such tremendous fear of sex that she unconsciously not only is content with Mr. Kenneth's impotence but even finds subtle ways of perpetuating that status quo of their sexual relationship. For example, when Mr. Kenneth does have an erection, she chooses that moment to quarrel about some trivial matter rather than to encourage him to try to use it for penetration. It is important that the counselor be nonjudgmental and understand that she behaves in this manner because of her own fears. The diagnostic thinking in the counselor's mind, upon which the treatment will be based, revolves around the understanding that both partners are more content than they are consciously aware with pregenital, predominantly oral forms of sex.

This case illustrates much about impotence and frigidity as they may be understood in depth. The foundation of Mr. Kenneth's impotence, speaking psychologically and developmentally, lies in oral, passive wishes. These prevent the adoption of an active, masculine sexual role. Developmental potential is released when the counselor succeeds in helping him know of these wishes as the first step toward helping him proceed beyond such points of fixation and regression. It would be a technical error to provide the patient with such information outside the context of a carefully established therapeutic relationship which includes transference and considerations of optimal timing of such interpretive work.

Mrs. Kenneth is also an orally fixated, dependent person. This common psychological ground forms the basis for the unconscious mutual attraction which made for the marriage in the first place. However, as we maintain throughout, the convergence of the problem has very little to do with how such individual fixations and regressions come about. Therefore, Mrs. Kenneth's life history and unconscious arrangements are in other respects different and must be treated with regard for these less obvious differences rather than for the more blatant similarities. Although Mrs. Kenneth helps in the perpetuation of the failure of consummation of the marriage because of her own fears and although this may make it appear as though she would be able to help Mr. Kenneth solve his problem if she could be more "cooperative," this is really the smallest part of the issue. Mrs. Kenneth is neither the cause of Mr. Kenneth's problem, nor can she be the cure of it. The ideal form of treatment would lessen her fears by enabling her to gain insight into her own difficulties in which they are based. If Mr. Kenneth's treatment, more or less, enables him simultaneously to become more active in his sexual performance, there will be a time of convergence when Mrs. Kenneth will be more receptive to his more masculine behavior. From such movement in the case and from the encouragement and incentive that would ensue from initial success, further development might be expected. The experienced counselor rarely expects such success in a straight line. More often than not, small degrees of success meet with increased amounts of anxiety, resulting in intensification of resistance and requiring that this be worked through before further steps forward are taken. The counselor who hopes for speedy and dramatic results will be prone to disappoint the patient and himself.

Referring once again to the Masters and Johnson technique, the Kenneth case appears to be an ideal one for fostering sexual "adjustment" by instructing the partners in methods that would work for them, at least mechanically. While it seems to us that this would not alter the oral bases of their personalities and that problems of dependency, inability to give gratification, incapacity to delay reasonably, problems in object relations, and the like, would remain untreated, there may be a place in the total treatment for educational procedures. However, potential danger in such mechanical adjustment exists for Mrs. Kenneth. Her fear of penetration is so great that the attempt to overcome her unconscious fantasies by fostering conscious acceptance of the act might lead to panic and personality disintegration. Another potential danger for the Kenneths lies in premature parenthood if consummation is attained before psychological growth. A third and related unfavorable potential is that the solution of the manifest difficulty, if successful, would deprive the couple of motivation for more profound solution. Nevertheless, it must be said that one of the goals of marital counseling is the furthering of satisfactory sex relations. It is conceivable, therefore, that a couple such as the Kenneths might be treated by a combination of psychological and educational methods which would include timing the mechanical intervention to coincide with the optimal moment of psychological readiness. Such treatment is, at present, in the area of proposed experimentation and would require carefully controlled study and followup before valid conclusions could be reached. We are only justified, for the time being, in describing the sexual problems of the cases under consideration in terms of the proved methods of psychological diagnosis and treatment.

The specific sexual difficulties and symptoms of the Alfreds, Charleses, Edwardses, and Kenneths are consistent with their broader psychological problems. The Bernards' problems suggest further elaboration. Mr. Bernard's sexual symptom is premature ejaculation, which occurs immediately upon intromission. He has essentially oral and anal psychosexual fixations; symbiotic wishes which are sometimes frank and sometimes defended against; and, particularly affecting his sexual behavior, limited capacity to postpone discharge. In the sex act, therefore, his capacity to wait extends long enough for intercourse to begin; at the next moment, however, it comes to an end. The oral interpretation is that he gives the partner a quick and unsatisfactory "feeding"; from the anal aspect, the withholding of gratification is more apparent; because of his symbiotic wishes, the desire to merge is present and is quickly counteracted by the defense against it—to get away quickly. Mrs. Bernard, unconsciously, does not mind this, although her conscious complaint is heard by the counselor. Her predominantly anal organization, to which she regresses as part of the "design" to prevent anxiety aroused by phallic-oedipal and even genital wishes, renders her relatively frigid for purposes of intercourse. Reconsidering her employment of reaction-formation as a defense, we see its effect upon her sexual functioning as operative; sex is confused, unconsciously, with dirtiness and therefore must be counteracted in the same way. Thus, in the manifest sexual behavior, Mrs. Bernard accepts the partial discharge attained by postcoital stimulation following Mr. Bernard's hasty ejaculation.

In this chapter, sexual symptoms that are characteristic of the total personality of the individual with the symptom have been examined. The varieties and combinations of interrelated personality and symptomatology are infinite and therefore cannot be detailed. In fact, some patients come for counseling with the understandable but erroneous impression that the experienced counselor has seen persons with similar problems before and that cure therefore is more rapidly attained because the road to understanding this particular individual is paved via the counselor's experience with another. Such expectation on the part of the patient is not borne out. The experienced counselor is most experienced in the *application* of diagnostic and technical skills toward the understanding of the individual's uniqueness. No two individuals, regardless of similarity of symptoms, are exactly alike. This is why even two partners in a marriage have to be treated individually. The same explanation holds for different patients who, although similar in some respects, have fundamentally different constitutional, environmental, and developmental equipment and experience. When counseling is addressed to understanding all aspects of these features of the personality, the treatment of the sexual problems per se will be seen within the broader context of psychoanalytic developmental psychology. It follows that when the total personality, via treatment or other developmental opportunity, proceeds to a higher level, sexual functioning usually improves along with it.

CHAPTER X

Marriage and the Life Cycle

THE fundamental implication in the developmental point of view is that potentiality for progressive growth is present throughout the life cycle. Until now, we have detailed the developmental tasks which normally precede marriage and which thereby constitute preparation for that event. Whether the selection of the partner is dictated by needs based upon regression and fixation; whether marriage constitutes a defensive arrangement; whether the choice of mate and the act of marriage represent growth-promoting and adaptive features in the personality; whether the marriage is phase-specific, all are considerations with which the preceding chapters are principally concerned. We also know (see Chapter I) that the act of entering into marriage is not necessarily an *indicator*, in the sense in which Spitz uses that term, of the attainment of a new level of integration which represents mastery of preceding developmental tasks. However, we have said that such may be true when earlier development has been completed successfully or even when some moderately uneven and pathological condition is provided with forward-thrusting impetus via the marital experience. Now let us consider the developmental features of the postwedding relationship, define some of the psychological challenges in an on-going marriage, and see how the developmental viewpoint enables the counselor to understand the critical phases in the life experience of later adulthood. In a certain sense, this chapter begins where the fairy tales leave off for, while married couples can and do live happily ever after, happiness is least likely to be attained when the experiences of daily living within marriage, which inevitably differ from the anticipatory fantasies which precede it, are not approached as developmental challenges. In no other aspect of living can it be so definitively stated:

> Still to ourselves in every place consigned,
> Our own felicity we make or find.

The most obvious task in the initial phase of marriage is that of sexual adjustment. Sex maintains its primary position as a developmental opportunity within marriage despite the increasing and more openly sanctioned premarital sexuality that is practiced today. In Chapters VI and IX, we discussed the effect of developmental problems upon the attainment of marital sexual adjustment. Here, for purpose of discussion, it will be taken for granted that both partners bring to the marriage "good enough" capacities to engage in mutually gratifying sex relations. We gain the advantage of presenting, at this point, some of the vicissitudes of more or less normal development through the life cycle in an on-going marriage (although we do intend to present and discuss pathological deviations from such norm).

Three major factors in human sexual adjustment require recapitulation here.

1. The biphasic onset of sexuality in the human being, which results in childhood sexuality and in the reemergence of sexuality in adolescence after the interim of sexual quiescence in the latency years

2. The incest taboo

3. The effect of object relations upon the "style" of sexual relatedness

The first two of these three uniquely human complexities in sexuality are inhibitory. The biphasic feature requires that the child postpone sexual fulfillment at least until consummation is biologically possible; social factors extend this time considerably in most instances. The incest taboo, whether regarded as related to or separate from the oedipus complex, is a universal prohibition which, with slight cultural variations, prevents consanguinity. Marriage, then, is called upon to provide a climate within which deeply ingrained prohibitions and inhibitions may be undone. No less powerful a combination than state, religion, and family, which had heretofore joined forces in the service of enforcement of prohibition, now reverse course and give sanction to sex in marriage. When such an impressive array of opponents becomes proponents, this change-about must derive its motivation from serious purpose. It is our suggestion that the purpose is the lending of full weight to lift the earlier taboo on sexuality and enable the young married couple to fulfill their adult roles in the community and in propagation. Such sanction, however powerful, is essentially sociologically oriented and helps the married couple only insofar as it provides the atmosphere within which the reversal of prohibition may take place. The psychological aspect, inhibition, is not appreciably lessened by the permissiveness of society, for, with all this external approval, the acceptance of sexuality depends entirely upon the internal unconscious approval of the individuals involved.

Internalization, including parental and societal prohibition, is attained with moderate and sometimes with great difficulty over a relatively long span of developmental time. With internalization as an essential process in development, we may see the relative ineffectiveness of prohibition or permission from without upon the behavior of the normal postadolescent young adult with an adequate superego. How, then, do young married couples overcome their sexual inhibitions? One supporting feature of this developmental process is that it is now phase-specific. Another, which is a factor that is always involved in a process, is that it takes time. Looking at the entire matter in more technical terms, we would say that certain ego and superego functions undergo alteration in the process of furthering sexual adjustment in marriage. On the ego side, this involves psychological as well as physical separation from oedipal objects and distinguishing the contemporary partner from them. (Mrs. Alfred, it will be recalled, failed in the separation task and Mrs. David in the oedipal one.) On the superego side, formerly prohibited or postponed behavior is now gradually sanctioned, aided by the awareness provided by the ego's reality testing that the sex partner is not an incestuous one. This brief recapitulation of the concept of internalization and its relevance in the gradual diminution and wearing-away of a powerful internalized restricting force explains in scientific terms what is readily observed in life— that living happily ever after does not come about magically nor even necessarily quickly. The social institution of the honeymoon, whereby the newly married couple has opportunity to be relieved of the responsibilities and distractions of daily living, provides an ideal climate and maximum psychic energy for internal reorganization. However, we know of no way of arranging honeymoon time to conform with the given couple's need. While one couple may make relatively good sexual adjustment in a matter of days, another couple may need months or even years.

The third aspect of sexual adaptation is concerned with the way in which sexual relatedness reflects the individual's level of object relations. Since the sex drive is so powerful, it is possible for it to attain discharge with or without the mediation of the ego. In some of the more extreme psychopathologies, the ego is not capable of directing the drive into suitable channels and so there can be rape or other nonobject related discharge. In normal and in less pathological conditions, sexual gratification includes another person who has to be taken into account in some way. In this regard, drive gratification and object relations are mutually enhancing. Much marital friction arises from the feeling that one is being used for need gratification only. Heard in the consultation room are complaints such as:

1. I exist for him only when he needs me for sex.
2. He is always too tired for it.
3. Nothing can satisfy her.
4. He never says that he loves me.
5. When she gets angry, that's the end of sexual relations for a long time.
6. She gives in when she wants something from me.

When drive gratification and object relations mesh together more smoothly because the level of object constancy prevails and the partner is valued independently of the need, marital friction is minimal. On a lesser or more fluctuating level of object relations, the complaints indicate the lag in development to which therapy should be addressed. The first complaint, for example, may be explored to clarify whether "I exist for him only. . . ." reflects the wife's own problems about identity and continuous existence, she has insatiable pregenital needs, or the husband does indeed use his wife's sexual apparatus for discharge of instinctual tension, without having reached the stage of object relations that enables him to value her. This example illustrates, too, the interlocking nature of problems in marriage. It is usually because there are growth lags in both partners that such problem constellations arise. In the third problem, the wife has herself not developed in some aspects of object relations nor matured beyond pregenital levels of drive organization; otherwise she would have been dissatisfied with the man who is now her husband when he was only a suitor. We suggest that problems involving object relations can be detected in the courtship period and do not arise only in the marriage bed. The point is even more emphatically made if, as is prevalent these days, there has been premarital sex. With or without premarital sexual relations, however, courtship patterns emerge. This man might very well have dated this woman only at his convenience, oblivious to her loneliness when he had no need to see her; he might have spent their dating time doing what he liked without regard for her likes and dislikes; he would have felt that she was making excessive demands if she had expressed some preferences of her own and that it would have entailed too much sacrifice for him. The woman who accepts such courtship behavior does so because it fits her unconscious need to be treated that way—masochistic need, for example. On the other side, this man would not have been able to continue to date a woman who placed demands upon him which exceeded his capacity to fulfill. He would have fled long before marriage. By the time such partners come to the marriage counselor, therefore, there is behind them a history of premarital acceptance of the behavior for which the spouse is now being blamed in the marriage. The clues which would have motivated one or both partners to terminate the relationship in the courtship period were not really overlooked, but were unconsciously perceived as desirable for pathological reasons.

Marital partners, however, do not often demonstrate to the counselor absolute failures in development. The very act of having married usually indicates at least some groping in the direction of object constancy. Most common in marital problems is that development of one or both spouses fluctuates between the extremes of need-gratifying object relations and an approach to object constancy. This is why a technical device known as *confrontation* (discussed more fully in Chapter XI) is tempting to use and is sometimes somewhat effective, at least temporarily. Confrontation means literally forcing the partner to face his behavior. However, it is often confrontation by the spouse which has brought him to the counselor in the first place. In the sixth complaint (She gives in when she wants something from me), the wife may come for counseling because the husband has confronted her with this, sometimes not very kindly. The fact that help is sought may be regarded as an indication that there is an unused reserve of growth potential, even if a small one. At the very least, the acceptance of the need for professional help includes some concern for the partner and for the marriage, even though this may be only concern to keep the partner in a need-gratifying role. Since there is rarely if ever total absence of adaptive capacity, given also a not too rigid defensive structure and a moderate but not too high degree of anxiety, the reserve potential *is* useful in promoting growth. It is also usable in technical short cuts such as confrontation because temporary change can sometimes be effected in this way by capitalizing on the concern for the partner, minimal as that might be. It is, however, our belief and experience that such movement, although sometimes useful, is limited because it leaves untapped the true growth potential and remains only a way of solving a specific crisis without preparing the partners to meet the next one. After the confrontation has produced an alteration in behavior, the tendency is to slip back to the existing level of object relations which is at the crux of the problem because, as we have said before, it is not possible for a person to function beyond his psychological capacity for prolonged periods of time even though the above-mentioned fluctuation makes it possible some of the time.

Another important area of initial, and sometimes of continuing, marital adjustment involves the reshaping of the relationship to the parents and the permanent departure from the parental home. This adjustment is mentioned in Chapter I as a developmental opportunity in that it includes yet another cycle of the separation process. Also, Mahler's concept of separation-individuation does not refer to physical separation, but rather to an internal process which involves the establishment of separate identity. While, in original development, the child's success in mastering separation-individuation depends to a large degree on the mother's behavior as "catalyst" of this process, the young adult is not or rather should not be similarly limited by the amount of assistance or encumbrance provided by the parents in the later round of separation-individuation which entering into marriage represents. Nevertheless, the problems of young and of no longer young married couples are laden with incomplete separation from the parents. Projection and rationalization are used often in these instances. "Mother looks forward all week to our coming for dinner regularly and I cannot bring myself to disappoint her" is one form such projection and rationalization takes. Often the telephone is used for maintaining daily and sometimes several-times-daily contact. In the Alfred case, Mrs. Alfred's mother was accepted as part of the necessary arrangement to keep the family functioning; Mr. Alfred would contend, consciously, that he is making the best of it, without awareness of his own need to have his mother-in-law there. Mrs. Lawrence, married twenty-five years and the mother of two nearly adult children, is still angry and complains to the counselor that her mother did not come to her home often enough to help with the care of the children when they were babies.

These examples of incomplete separation-individuation after marriage are not designed to imply that the external criteria of how much time, devotion, and interest centered in the parents provide much diagnostic clue to the state of separation, nor are they used to imply that the relationship with the parents comes to an end when marriage takes place. Rather, a gradual process of separation-individuation, which reaches its first milestone at about the age of three years, continues, repeats, and reinforces itself throughout life. Looked at in this way, life is a series of external separations which support the internal process—birth, weaning, nursery school, grade school with longer hours, parents going out together, summer camp, adolescence, college away from home, and sometimes one's own apartment—tend to aid separation-individuation and often constitute indicators of how that process is proceeding. Marriage, however, provides an altogether different medium for such development. In all other instances cited, the parental home still remains *home base;* it is a security backstop to which one can always return. In marriage, there is a statement of intention to give up the parental home and to establish a home of one's own, with a partner with whom one has also to establish an on-going, permanent relationship. It is this latter quality which makes marriage different even from the departure from the parental home and the establishment of one's own apartment by the unmarried adult.

In review, we see that marriage constitutes a developmental phase which integrates past developmental accomplishments, welding them together into a new structure which becomes the preparatory step toward the next developmental phase. It is evident that all previously accomplished separations contribute to the success of the psychological departure from the parental home at the point of marriage. The well-known going "home to mother" by the frightened bride is an obvious indication that separation-individuation in marriage has failed because prior separations have not succeeded.

More frequently encountered in marital counseling is not the complete reversal of the marital step by returning to mother but rather an in-between state in which the married man or woman is torn between parental obligation and marital home. This was true of Mrs. Lawrence, who still, after so many years of marriage, continues the pattern of visiting her mother several times a week under the pretext that her mother is getting old and needs her help in keeping house. Thus, she deals with the resentment about mother not having helped her when she needed it by doing now what she felt mother should have done years ago. The concept of differentiation of self representations from object representations supplements that of separation-individuation in enabling the counselor to understand these problems and to establish therapeutic goals. It is never the goal literally to separate the patient from his parent. Mrs. Lawrence is confused because she sees her mother and herself, unconsciously, too much as the same and so she behaves as she believes her mother would, or should. When the counselor helps her begin to differentiate so that she can say, "This is the way mother is, but that is the way I am," some steps toward more sharply delineating self representations from object representations have taken place and Mrs. Lawrence will, spontaneously, alter her behavior toward her mother and, inevitably, toward husband and children as well. This level of therapy may be compared with the logical-sounding attempt to add up numbers of hours spent with mother versus the number spent with marital family; while it appears sensible, such logic does not reach the unconscious. Mrs. Lawrence needs the therapist's help in the fundamental matter of establishment of an identity separate from that of her mother and, when this succeeds, advice about how to spend her time becomes superfluous.

The entire burden of our point of view rests on the theory that separation-individuation and differentiation of self representations from object representations are internal processes. We have already said that literal termination of the relationship with the parents is not the goal, and to this we might add that such a goal may not even be desirable. When termination does take place, it is usually in anger and always because the attempt is being made to deal with incomplete internal separation via external arrangements that provide the appearance of "independence." What does change, desirably, when the adult-child marries, is the *quality* of the relationship with the parents. Gradual separation-individuation frees neutralized libidinous and aggressive energy for age-appropriate tasks. Earlier in life, this provides the ego with energy for education and the attainment of skills; in marriage, such energy becomes available for the establishment of new and lasting relationships with spouse and later with children. So far as the parents are concerned, because object constancy remains, they continue to be loved persons who, nevertheless, lead their own lives with separate and sometimes converging interests.

Problems revolving around separation from the parental home become even more complex when there are financial considerations, as in the case of a son who may wish to marry but whose parents really need his financial support. There are no clear-cut formulae for the solution of reality problems. It can only be said that solutions are more readily worked out when the psychological aspect lends minimal complexity. To a somewhat less intense degree, similar separation tasks are involved in the attenuation of the intensity of premarital friendships after marriage. Damon and Pythias cannot maintain the same closeness after the marriage of either. It is implicit in normal development that heterosexuality will dominate the libidinal drive and will dictate a different relationship with friends of the same sex. With regard to the problem of separation from parents and friends, the reference here is to shift in basic loyalty from them to the spouse; parental relationships and friendships remain, but mold themselves to the new situation.

The familiar mother-in-law problem warrants mention only here; later, it is discussed from the side of the aging mother. That such problems stem from incomplete separation-individuation of adult son or daughter and mother is evident. Also evident is the fact that a man or woman who has not completed separation from his or her own mother will find more courage in fighting it out with the mother-in-law. This very common type of "mother-in-law trouble" may be understood as representing the unresolved struggle of the adolescent who employs the aggressive drive in the service of separation-individuation. Though age-appropriate in adolescence, it is, of course, "out of place" in marriage. The counselor, understanding this, will then deal with it as with any other aspect of incompletion of development.

We now come to the more sociologically flavored factor of "role." With the successful accomplishment of developmental, that is, intrapsychic, tasks, a man fulfills with ease the role of husband, provider, father, and member of the community; a woman accepts and welcomes biology's dictate that she bear and nurture the children and psychology's dictate that she lend herself to their changing phase-specific needs. Particularly in the early months of a child's life, fathering means providing the setting within which the mother can perform her maternal tasks. In a recent and most significant study of the role of the pre-oedipal father, Greenacre describes him from the infant's-eye view as a dimly sensed, twilight figure until approximately the beginning of the second year of life when he emerges as a glorious, idealized, and somewhat mysterious person who is away much of the time, but who, when present, has a direct and important impact upon the child. His more active tossing, romping, and generally more muscular involvement with the child at this age offers an experience quite different from that with the mother. Mahler and Greenacre agree that this paternal experience provides the child with direct and vital assistance in the beginning separation-individuation process that is phase-specific at this time. It is observable that children without fathers tend to cling more to mother, and Greenacre's elaboration of the role of the father in the second year of life contributes elegantly to our understanding of the importance of his presence.

Just as marriage inevitably alters the equilibrium between parent and adult child, the arrival of the first child in a marriage alters the equilibrium between husband and wife; the dyad becomes a triad. If the above-described role acceptance is adequate, the new equilibrium is established more smoothly than otherwise. No such major shift in external and internal equilibrium can be expected to take place without some upheaval. As in adolescence, absence of upheaval in this phase, too, would indicate that the progressive, developmental shifts are not taking place.

The more common failures in acceptance of parenthood lead us to look first at the father whose phase-specific task is to provide masculine balance to the triad, actual and psychological support to the mother. If his maternal identification is too great, the arrival of a baby may become an opportunity for the fulfillment of feminine wishes under the guise of helping in the care of the baby. This can only be discussed in terms of internal processes rather than of actual activity because, as we have already said about time and other such external factors, quantitative measurement of activity is not possible, nor would it avail much if it were. A man can do much of the work or little or none at all, without any of these in and of themselves constituting much guide to the internal acceptance of the paternal role. He may, if defense against feminine, maternal wishes are reinforced by the arrival of a baby, turn entirely in the other direction and ignore the child altogether. Sometimes such defensive behavior is interpreted as sibling rivalry, as oedipal rivalry if the baby is a boy, as reactivation of castration anxiety if the baby is a girl. While it may be any or even all of these, diagnostic distinction must be made. To these possibilities we might add the previously discussed separation anxiety and need-gratifying level of object relations.

Also to be considered is the reactivization of pregenital wishes in identification with the baby, particularly orality in the first months of the baby's life. Whether these potential danger points create much or little upheaval in the marriage depends not only upon their degree but also upon whether earlier phases of development lend enough strength to the forward thrust imposed by this new developmental phase.

The wife who becomes a mother is also dependent in her psychological acceptance of the new role upon the legacy provided by earlier development. For her, regression to symbiotic union with the baby is appropriate, but involves a potential problem if the regression does not serve the ego and becomes either too much of a good thing or its opposite—avoided because of anxiety about and therefore defense against such regression. Concomitant regression to orality is not desirable and it is in such areas that distinction must be made between the ego and the instinctual drives, for the mother must feed the child and feel at one with him without herself needing to be fed in the same way. Here, phase-specific attunement may be elaborated to mean that she senses the clues provided by the child in his developmentally changing needs and responds accordingly. Her flexibility in this regard leans heavily upon her own earlier development.

This very brief description of the early mothering role suffices to distinguish the different psychological demand upon the man and woman in the beginning phase of parenthood. It demonstrates that there is a somewhat greater demand upon the woman in that a more total immersion in parenthood is required of the mother than of the father at first. Not all women can tolerate so much withdrawal from adult pursuits. Although masculine strivings play a role here, and might very well cause a problem in a woman such as Mrs. Charles, such strivings do not account altogether for the complexity of the conflicts which a new mother may experience. Especially, if a woman is to have several children, her role as mother occupies some of the most valuable years of her adulthood and conflicts in varying degrees with other needs, wishes, and interests. The continuously changing role of women in modern society adds to the problems of acceptance of motherhood, but need not impair this function. Childbearing and child rearing, it is true, may disrupt educational, vocational, and professional activity, social life, community work, and the like. There is no single solution to these interrelated psychological and sociological problems. Each woman finds her own solution. For one, satisfaction may be complete in being mother and housewife; for another, activities vary with the changing needs of the children, and the roles of mother, wife, and career woman can be agreeably combined; for still another, there may be dissatisfaction and disharmony to such a degree that other solutions will have to be worked out. It is our thought in this regard that the capacity for adaptation is of outstanding importance in determining the outcome of the woman's acceptance of motherhood and of her adjustment to it. In a less sophisticated era, therapists used to ask the troubled mother of a troubled child whether the child had been wanted. We know now that conscious wanting of a child can mean many different things, as exemplified by Mrs. Charles, and that it is the least of the matter. We also know that anticipation of an event and the reality of the event itself cannot altogether coincide and that adaptation has to be made step by step or, put more simply, bridges can only be crossed when one comes to them. For the counselor who is called upon to help a new mother adapt to or accept maternity, it is useful to know that the child needs maternal availability for the development of adequate psychic structure. How the counselor helps her work this out includes, as the essential core of counseling, consideration of her own developmental and adaptive potential.

An aspect of parenthood which affects man and woman with equal intensity is the acceptance of membership in the older generation. While, via identification, the parent does to some extent relive his own childhood in the vicarious enjoyment of the child's development, this is favorable only if limited. The child's unabashed instinctual needs may draw the parent into regression in the unconscious attempt to gain gratification which is no longer phase-specific for the parent. Though the counselor may be understanding of the fact that this regression occurs because there had been deprivations in the parent's own childhood, he will also understand its inappropriateness now. Sometimes counseling is needed to help the parent shift more sharply from the role of receiver to that of provider; if these roles are blurred, there is confusion between the generations. Sometimes the problem lies in the fact that the parent has, again unconsciously, invested the child with his own unfulfilled fantasies. Since parent-child counseling is beyond our scope here, we limit this discussion to consideration of the necessity for maintaining the gap between generations. Parents who are clear about their position in this regard are best able to foster the processes of internalization explained in Chapter VII. They are, at the same time, in the best position to exploit and enjoy their own developmental opportunities as they shift from young to middle adulthood, to middle age and to old age. A parent can be a "pal" to the child to a very limited extent only, if both are to attain developmental success. Parents and children should not be involved in sharing of sexual knowledge about one another, nor in less "loaded" intimacies, lest such erasure of the difference between generations impair the success of the phase-specific tasks which differ for each. The child's basic developmental tasks are to acquire psychic structure, including identity, independent skills, education, experience in peer relationships. The child needs to resolve oedipal wishes and to accept exclusion from the parental sexual relationship in order to be free to become, in turn, a member of the parent generation. The parent's developmental tasks, at the same time, involve his or her own establishment in gender role, vocational arrangements, and object relations with spouse. These vastly different tasks of parent and child are impaired if there is too much "palship" and an equality which can only be false because no child is psychologically ready for it. The benign authority of the parental role is the ideal climate within which parent and child maintain clarity about who they are and what is to be expected of each. At no time in life can this difference between generations be usefully overcome. Even when the children become adults and parents in their own right, although the gap narrows somewhat, it never disappears.

It is usually during the years of early parenthood that the husband and father is engaged in establishing himself in his vocation, business, or profession. This is an important developmental phase for him and a particular reaffirmation of his adequacy and masculinity. Social workers, probably more than any other professional group, are familiar with the psychological problems which ensue from failure to attain success as a provider, whether because of one's own problems or because of external disaster such as war, economic depression, unemployment, racial discrimination, or the like. Mr. Harold, in Chapter VII, illustrates that psychological breakdown can occur without sociological aggravation, but at this point we wish to affirm that national and international disaster can exacerbate individual developmental problems, even though we do not regard elaboration of the vicissitudes of such events to be within the scope of our detailed consideration of marriage.

The ordinary events of the child's growth from an infant to a schoolchild do not usually present important crises in marriage. Even the passing of the oedipal phase, so eventful for the child, is not usually of great significance in the marriage unless the parents have been pathologically involved in it. When the child reaches puberty and enters adolescence, however, potentiality for disequilibrium increases. The reawakening of the child's sexual instincts, his struggle to cope with these, his increasing desire for and inexperience with independence, and particularly his noisy projection of these internal struggles upon the parents can constitute a strain which even the most patient parents find difficult. To this must be added the adolescent's reawakened oedipal conflict, which usually takes its toll on each parent in different ways, aggression turning more markedly toward the parent of the same sex. The parents' level of object relations and degree of neutralization of counteraggression are not only put to the test but are provided, if looked at more positively, with one more opportunity to rise to higher levels. Thus, the child's developmental phase, adolescence, can, with or without counseling, constitute another developmental chance for the parents.

An added critical factor in the parents' development intrudes when the child or children reach adolescence. By this time the parents are some twenty years older than when they married and are nearer confrontation with their own aging processes. When object constancy obtains and constitutes a central thread in the marital relationship, the awareness that oneself and one's spouse are no longer young and beautiful can lead to yet another development in the life cycle; when this thread is weak, it can lead to upheaval, quarreling, and the well-known last extramarital fling in the desperate attempt to stave off the acceptance of middle age. Sometimes, the adolescence of the child may stir up resurgence of the parent's adolescent narcissistic fantasies which obviously do not correspond to the realities of phase-specificity for the parent. This is one of the phases in the life cycle when divorce and remarriage are sought as solutions, as though youth can be regained in a new marriage.

The mother of the adolescent or adult child is likely to be dealing also with menopausal changes which have both physiological and psychological impact. Hormonal imbalance leads to physical distress and, depending upon her characteristic way of using illness, may have varying effects upon the marital relationship. The psychological concomitants may be even more disturbing, not only because aging cannot be denied but because cessation of menses contains potentiality for revival of unconscious, unfulfilled fantasies. Often, realization of the incapacity to bear more children leads to depressive reactions. If we can imagine Mrs. Charles in middle age, she might be seen as a person who, without treatment, might succumb to a menopausal depression.

During this time, too, the grandparents of the adolescent child are reaching the end of their lives. One or both spouses might then be in mourning for his and her own parents, including reactivization of the separation anxiety which the finality of death imposes. Depending upon what the relationship to the parents had been, the middle-aged spouse would, upon bereavement, experience grief, guilt, depression, all of which would have their effect upon the marriage in direct correlation with the degree of deviation from normal mourning. Before the death of the aged parents, there is sometimes involvement with them because of financial need, illness, and the infirmities of age; these are bound to reactivate unresolved problems in the middle-aged son or daughter and to deflect from the marital relationship, at least temporarily. Again, how this is dealt with depends upon level of development, perhaps especially of object relations.

When the last adolescent child reaches young adulthood and leaves home, the marital partners are alone together. Their roles as parents are completed for all necessary purposes after they have "catalyzed" their children's adulthood and independence. Failure to fulfill this function is so well known that we need not describe in detail the parent who "hangs on"—the mother who cannot approve of her son's choice of a wife; the father who cannot enable the son to make an independent vocational choice. Sometimes the clinging parent and the unseparated-unindividuated adult child remain together for life. More often, however, the son or daughter does marry or leaves home without or before marrying. At any rate, the moment of being alone together as an aging couple comes to many. Again, this can be a crisis which will threaten the marriage or it can be a developmental opportunity. How it is experienced depends largely upon whether the married couple have regarded parenthood as an important but nevertheless terminable phase in life. If they have not faced its termination, they may find themselves psychologically "unemployed" when the children grow up and leave. They no longer have much of a future and the present becomes of supreme importance. At this stage, counseling is often useful in helping them find new interests if their lives have revolved too much around the children. Some aging couples regard the "unemployment" as only temporary and eagerly await the arrival of grandchildren. While this is a joyous event in the lives of the couple, if they use it for "reemployment" they are likely to become too reinvolved with their children and grandchildren. Often, "mother-in-law" trouble begins again with the young couple's struggle to keep the grandmother from taking over too much. Under ideal conditions, the older couple will have found new interests and peer relationships, will enjoy visits with children and grandchildren, but will have employed their own developmental opportunities so well that they can allow their adult married children to work out their phase-specific developmental tasks of marriage and parenthood without interference.

When the older couple is alone and the man retires, the lifelong anticipated leisure may be fulfilling or it may be disappointing. The outcome depends not only upon how earlier developmental opportunities have been employed but upon whether the anticipatory fantasies were close enough to reality so that the gap is not too great. By this time of life, the wife, even if she has not worked outside the home, has her routine and sometimes finds the daily presence of the husband less enjoyable than was anticipated. Unless the leisure is planned for psychologically as well as practically, the time may be spent in quarreling rather than in the enjoyment of the rewards of a lifetime of productive work.

The death of a spouse is a profoundly difficult event. The loss of companionship, sexual partner, provider, homemaker reflect losses in areas of interaction. Painful as these may be, such functions are replaceable. It is the experience of internal loss of a cathected object that is the most painful and that involves the "work" of mourning; that is, withdrawing the investment of psychic energy from the internal representation of the deceased spouse because he or she no longer exists and the survivor has to go on living. If the loss occurs early in the marriage, while there are still young children, the problems of child rearing and of earning a living enormously complicate the mourning process. Finally, the last years of life may have to be spent in widowhood, in loneliness, and in some degree of infirmity. The developmental point of view lends dimension to the counselor's understanding that the capacity to cope with life's rewards and tragedies begins to be established early in life and, if adequately built and reworked throughout the developmental phases of adulthood, increases in strength.

CHAPTER XI

Technical and Diagnostic Considerations in Marital Counseling

REFERENCE to a technique of marital counseling implies that there is a specific approach unique to the treatment of marital problems. This is correct to a limited extent only, for if marital counseling is defined as the treatment of individuals who present themselves for therapy at a particular starting point, it is only at the initial phase that some difference from general psychotherapy exists. Even in this opening phase, insofar as such manner of presentation of the problem constitutes a form of resistance, it may be said that there is no difference between marital counseling and psychotherapy because resistance is a feature of all psychotherapy and of psychoanalysis as well. The psychoanalytic patient, after declaration of the desire to be analyzed, characteristically backs away from that consciously stated intention at many points in the course of his treatment; the patient who is being treated by psychoanalytically oriented forms of psychotherapy displays similar resistance.

The classical definition of *resistance* is the employment of defense in the therapeutic situation. We referred earlier to the fact that some of the scientific terms in psychoanalytic theory are borrowed from the common vocabulary. *Resistance* is one of these and, if defined in its ordinary sense, lends itself to technical misunderstanding. It is not, as the patient is wont to think, deliberate sabotaging of the treatment; it is rather the characteristic way in which the individual deals with anxiety and, as such, needs to be respected as necessary to him until the anxiety is reduced.

It is stated in the Introduction that persons with marital problems employ the defense mechanisms of projection and displacement to a large degree; to this it is useful to elaborate that the initial resistance, therefore, includes lack of insight and self-awareness, as well as the tendency to regard the problem as interrelated. More often than not, there is also a very marked tendency to derive unconscious gratification from the neurotic interaction in the marriage. Most of our case material illustrates that, while counseling is sought because discomfort is experienced consciously, the partners are unaware of and loathe to relinquish unconscious pleasure which is pertinent to their level of development. Mr. and Mrs. Alfred, for example, found oral satisfaction in their marital arrangement; the Bernards unconsciously "enjoyed" the sado-masochistic interaction; the Charleses employed unconscious phallic teasing; the Davids had a comfortable father-child arrangement; the Edwardses needed the symbiotic closeness even though it troubled them to the extent that they also wanted separation; Mr. and Mrs. Frank wanted to be "good" objects to each other and were consciously as well as unconsciously reluctant to give up trying to be so impossibly perfect; Mr. and Mrs. George had an unconscious "pact" that he would be the provider and that sexual responsiveness would constitute an undesirable impediment; the Harolds needed each other to bolster identity; Mr. and Mrs. James needed the maternal care that, in reality, adults cannot provide successfully for one another; the Kenneths unconsciously preferred pregenital sexuality to such an extent that genital contact was precluded; Mr. and Mrs. Lawrence acted out their unresolved separation from their own mothers, Mrs. Lawrence by attending her mother, Mr. Lawrence by "understanding" the necessity for this via identification. The concept of unconscious gratification is well known to the psychoanalytic psychotherapist and need not be elaborated here, especially in the details of technical considerations about which a large literature exists.

There is less knowledge about the techniques of dealing with the person who is deficient in the major qualification for becoming a patient—awareness of problem within himself. How, then, does the marriage counselor deal with the marital partner who comes for treatment thinking that the problem lies in the marriage, that it is usually the spouse who is at fault, that therefore life would be happier if the spouse were to change his personality, and that the counselor is equipped to provide an immediate and omniscient solution? Some therapists dismiss such persons as untreatable or suggest that they return for treatment when they acquire some awareness of problem. The latter suggestion does not always turn out to be as impossible as it appears because, in some instances, the vicissitudes of life force self-awareness upon the person and he does return for treatment when some real crisis occurs. Nevertheless, the inherent fallacy in such suggestion is evident, and that is why we are here proposing the kinds of techniques that enable the "resistant" marital partner to become a patient in his own right. One of the most commonly employed techniques involves the concept of accepting the patient "where he is." For some counselors this means that, since the marital partner places his perception of the problem in the area of the interaction, it is the interaction that should be the focus of treatment. We interpret this concept in a somewhat different way, namely, that while the patient does have to be heard in his own terms, especially in the beginning, this does not dictate the ultimate course of treatment. Treatment, we have maintained in the earlier chapters, must be based upon the diagnostic considerations which we have outlined, not upon what the patient consciously thinks he wants or needs. This does not mean that one refutes or disregards his wishes, but only that the counselor realizes that counselor and patient begin together on the surface (that is, as the patient sees things) and the counselor, aware of the many other factors involved, leads the patient gradually into greater depth. In the beginning, therefore, the counselor does several sometimes paradoxical things at once.

1. He identifies with the patient in order to be able to see the problem as the patient sees it, but remains sufficiently objective to diagnose and to note those factors which appear to exist only in the present but really becloud the present because they contain within them distortions from the past.

2. He bears in mind that the partners have come to try to protect their marriage, and so he lends himself to that purpose as well as to the consciously stated dissatisfactions and the unconscious gratifications in the status quo.

3. He sometimes yields to the wishes of the spouses that they be seen together in the beginning, because this is the only way in which they can begin, but is always mindful that it is usually more desirable for them to have separate counselors. When both spouses have to be seen by the same counselor, he is called upon to identify with not one but two different persons and yet maintain a stance of neutrality in their struggle.

4. He avoids using his experience omnisciently even when his greater knowledge, skill, intuitive gifts, wisdom, and the like may be considerable; if the developmental framework has meaning, it dictates that the counselor's role is to help the individual attain autonomy and arrive at his own solutions after movement within the counseling situation succeeds in correcting developmental defects.

Thus, the counselor must have the capacity to work on various levels from the elementary one of providing opportunity for ventilation, to diagnosis and definition of the problem, to moving it out of the area of interaction into its intrapsychic origins, to enabling the patient to arrive at insight and self-awareness when this proves possible. Much counseling can and does terminate quite validly when the marriage is no longer the arena of struggle; *transference* is the invaluable technical tool whereby this is accomplished. Given the assumption that the mode of relatedness to another person is indicative of the individual's level of development, it can be expected that this same mode will be as operative in the relationship with the counselor as with the spouse and others. If the transference is employed, therefore, to provide insight into the patient's characteristic way of relating, the patient is gradually enabled to see that part in the marital interaction which constitutes his contribution to the disharmony, and he may be motivated to modify or to withdraw it. When the patient, in the transference relationship with the counselor, begins to see that he distorts the counselor's statements, attitudes, and behavior in a way that duplicates features of the marital interaction, a good therapeutic stride has taken place. A new level of insight has been attained in that the patient has begun to understand that there exists a common denominator within him which distorts in both relationships. This common denominator or basic model within himself is the prototypical relationship to the significant objects in his childhood. Here, the treatment has moved from initial projection and displacement to insight.

The concept of transference is, of course, well known in the technique of psychoanalysis. Although it is not always employed in some forms of psychotherapy, the developmental point of view dictates its use whenever possible. Occasions when it may not be possible include brief contact, when the time for the establishment of a firm transference is not availble, or when the patient is so disturbed in his ego functions, particularly object relations and reality testing, that too-distorted transference is likely to obscure reality. By and large, however, transference is usable and becomes solidified with time; thus absence of haste is one of the more cogent technical considerations in this regard. By definition, *transference* is the repetition in the present of unconscious feelings toward important figures from childhood and is not limited to the therapeutic situation. Physicians, dentists, lawyers, teachers, and similar professional persons are familiar with the phenomenon whereby feelings develop because the individual finds himself or herself in a position of need which reactivates the helpless, dependent feelings of childhood, the love and aggression, and displaces them upon the person whose help is sought in the present. It is only in psychoanalysis and psychotherapy, however, that this phenomenon has been appreciated thoroughly as the central therapeutic tool that brings the patient into a psychological position which enables the therapist to help the patient understand and overcome those feelings which belong to the past.* After the patient has become able to discern that he deals with the counselor as he does with his wife and that such behavior is dictated by feelings that he had toward his father or mother at a particular time in his childhood—in other words, when he has reached the comprehension that the common factor in his contribution to the marital interaction is not the seeming similarity in the behavior of his object, but in feelings within himself—he has taken a large step. The rational part of his ego has been stimulated to look within, rather than at what spouse and others are doing to him and insight becomes possible.

This is an appropriate place for us to elaborate on the technical device known as *confrontation,* discussion of which began in Chapter X. Although it is frequently practiced with

---

* It was Freud's courage and integrity as well as his genius that caused him to recognize transference as the valuable therapeutic tool that it is, whereas his collaborator, Breuer, abandoned psychoanalytic investigation when his patient developed feelings toward him in the course of treatment.

a different technical meaning and intent,* we define confrontation as insight gained when the reasonable, observing aspect of the person's ego is able to "look at" the experiencing part and confront himself *intrasystemically* (within his own ego). While the most obvious advantage of such internal confrontation is that the patient is less likely to refute and reject internally perceived understanding of himself, this is not necessarily the greater advantage. The most valuable aspect of confrontation from within is that such insight in and of itself is therapeutic in the sense that it promotes autonomy and ego growth, two interrelated aspects of development which can only be "catalyzed" but never imposed from without. It is for this reason that we say in Chapter X that, while confrontation by spouse, therapist, or others, may be somewhat effective, it cannot be growth-promoting.

When the transference is firmly established and the ego is strengthened via self-confrontation, the next important step in treatment is the diminution or even cessation of the neurotic interaction. This is not only the prime opportunity for the removal of the marriage from the arena of struggle, which we believe to be a valuable outcome of marital counseling in and of itself, but it often also provides progressive opportunity by depriving the interpersonal aspects of the marriage of their more infantile forms of pleasure. Bearing in mind that the unconscious aspects of the interrelatedness are often more pleasurable than is consciously recognized, the moment may arrive, in counseling, when the pleasure is given up for the sake of making room for more mature types of gratification. This very interesting aspect of growth-promotion in treatment has sometimes been misunderstood, even among psychotherapists, because the rather unfortunate term *abstinence* is used

---

* That is, as a presentation from without by spouse, therapist, therapy group members, or others, all of whom are sources which do not in any way coincide with the patient's own ego function of self-observation.

to designate it as a technical device. The unpleasant connotation of the word, however, need not deter us from appreciation of its true meaning and value. *Abstinence* means the deliberate avoidance of *infantile* gratification both within and, at appropriate times, outside the therapeutic situation. In marital counseling, it may often mean that the spouse gives up the growth-inhibiting interaction, such as sado-masochistic provocation and attack, so that more mature, age-appropriate forms of gratification may replace it. Even if only one partner no longer joins in, the interaction ceases or diminishes, and this would, at the very least, have some beneficial effect upon the relationship, if it serves only to decrease the quarreling. If there are children, it provides a more peaceful climate for their own growth.

Abstinence within the treatment situation means that the counselor does not gratify all the demands of the patient and it is in this area that the professional authority of the counselor comes into play. We said that he must begin by identifying with the patient in order to understand him. This kind of identification includes benign withholding of gratifications that would be detrimental to growth. It is not as severe as its exposition makes it appear, because the very fact that the patient has an interested listener is, in and of itself, a gratification, but one that is consistent with the therapeutic relationship. This subtle aspect of technique is reassuring to the beginning therapist, who may have the wish to provide as much as possible for the patient without realizing that he is already providing a great deal.

Consider now some of the other features that the therapist's professional stance involve.

1. The counselor must himself possess enough self-awareness to be able to distinguish the perception of his own problems from those of the patient. In psychoanalytic language, the concept of *countertransference* is involved here. For purposes

of counseling, we confine our consideration of this matter to clarification that the counselor's objectivity must include the ability to keep his own problems, feelings, biases, and the like, away from the patient. Freud's instructions in this regard have sometimes been misunderstood and quoted out of context, although he writes clearly enough about them. He describes the therapeutic stance as designed solely for the patient's benefit; although this has been misinterpreted to mean that the therapist should be cold, detached, and unfeeling, it only means that he should ensure that gratification of his own needs does not impair the therapeutic contact. The implication here is that, although warmth, empathy, and the capacity to identify are essential in understanding the patient, interaction between therapist and patient is contraindicated if its unconscious design is in the service of the therapist's pleasure. From this it follows that the counselor is a *professional* in the full sense of the word—he professes to use special knowledge and skill to offer a service which the nonprofessional cannot perform. For this purpose, he must himself be possessed of a level of self-awareness which would preclude conscious or unconscious seeking of gratification of his own needs in his relationship with the patient. Although we cannot discuss here the various unconscious elements which dictate choice of profession, it is at least possible to say that the motivation for such choice contains within it both conscious and unconscious consideration that there will be gratification in it. The therapist's daily work must be pleasurable to him or he would not be able to engage in it. If, as is often the case, these gratifications happen to coincide with the patient's need for insight and promotion of growth, well and good; if, however, the needs of the patient happen not to be pleasurable for the therapist, he should have the capacity to forgo gratification of his own needs in that situation. Since some of the needs may be unconscious, many therapists choose to have personal psychotherapy or psychoanalysis as part of their preparation for the practice of this very personally demanding profession.

2. Related to objectivity is the stance of neutrality. Neutrality involves absence of moral judgment, authoritarianism, decision-making, and stake in the specific outcome of the treatment. While this, too, seems paradoxical, it is at the same time rather evident that the best outcome is that the patient acquires independence and autonomy; in that sense, therefore, the therapist's neutrality best assures that the patient will make his own decision about his life. This attitude is of particular importance in marital counseling when two spouses, and often children as well, are involved, and one can all too easily be tempted to think that one knows what is best for all or, worse than that, become overidentified with one family member against another.

3. Attitudes of omniscience are to be avoided. This is stressed here as part of the therapist's general professional equipment because there is much confusion about this matter. Some theoreticians regard intuition as a prime technical tool. While we agree with the thought that the capacity to empathize is an essential feature of the therapist's talent for his profession, that some persons are more intuitive than others, and that such talent can be valuable, we do not regard the employment of the therapist's insights as useful if conveyed to the patient as an exercise of the therapist's powers. Although sometimes such so-called intuitive interpretive activity constitutes a tour de force which can be very impressive, it has little therapeutic value because it exercises the therapist's rather than the patient's ego functions and skills. In this respect it operates contrary to the developmental point of view which advocates that the patient be led to greater and greater levels of independence. At its most detrimental, it can frighten the symbiotic, unseparated patient, whose absence of individual identity leads him to fear that his mind is being read when the

therapist provides intuitive thoughts, correct as these might be.

We wish to enumerate some of the many factors which enter into the therapist's particular way of listening to the patient. While "listening" has been discussed, sometimes humorously, often as an oversimplified description of what the psychotherapist does, our conceptualization of the process conveys that it is a far more active one than is commonly thought. In listening, the therapist

1. hears the patient's manifest statements

2. maintains a respectful attitude that what the patient has to say is worth listening to

3. minimizes interruptions

4. frees himself from overconcern, excessive sympathy, excessive coldness, excessive anxiety

5. avoids holding out promises of cure, within an encouraging climate

6. identifies with the patient and understands his dilemma

7. maintains an open-minded curiosity which encourages the patient to provide more and more information in a welcoming atmosphere

8. discerns the unconscious threads in the patient's productions and tries to understand the deeper layers of the problem

9. notices the meaningful emotional tones and affects

10. hears the transference manifestations that make it possible to know the effect of past feelings upon the present situation

11. remains alert to diagnostic clues

12. seeks the truth, even when it must emerge, as it often does, in having to listen to unpleasant statements about himself

13. tries to enlist the patient's ego in joining with his own toward the therapeutic goal

14. withholds his own moral, political, religious, social and personal bias

The technique of treatment is most adequately performed within the guidelines of proper diagnosis. In the foregoing chapters, we have described the diagnostic considerations that are indicated by maturational and developmental aspects of the psychological growth processes. We have employed, in particular, knowledge gained about development of the ego and its functions in the last two decades, integrating this with the earlier knowledge provided by instinct theory to an understanding of marriage as a developmental phase. Typical problems in the failure of development at this phase have been described. We now add a recapitulation in the form of a diagrammatic scheme of maturation and development as a guide to diagnosis. This scheme shows how maturation and development proceed in parallel, interrelate, sometimes converge, and also how unevenness in development and maturation, particularly if such unevenness is very great, imposes sometimes insuperable tasks upon psychological growth.

The vertical columns schematize the various aspects of maturation and development beginning with the earliest stages of life and proceeding in the direction of higher levels down the length of the columns. The first three columns refer to the Id and include psychosexual maturation and drive differentiation. The columns concerned with the Ego include Object Relations, Processes of Internalization, Taming of the Drives, Symbiosis and Separation-Individuation, Level of Anxiety, Defenses; they also indicate where the potentiality for defects and distortions in ego development are likely to arise. The last column refers to Superego formation and describes schematically the archaic precursors of this part of the psychic structure and how these gradually develop into an internalized regulator of behavior. Finally, we illustrate the diagnostic use of such a diagram by recapitulation of the case of Mrs. Alfred, comparing her with Mrs. Bernard.

Mrs. Alfred is fixated on the oral level (see line 17 in column 1). Drive differentiation is incomplete, as is the capacity to delay gratification (see columns 2, 3, and 4). Object relations are on the level of need-gratification (column 4) and the diagram enables us to note how this coincides with inadequate neutralization (column 6) and with failure to have attained separation-individuation—psychological birth—(column 7). Her level of anxiety involves fear of loss of the object and fear of merger (column 8). Defenses (column 9) are primitive and include introjection, projection and denial, such relatively unsophisticated defensive organization being consistent with an inadequate level of ego development in general and with the incapacity to employ anxiety as a signal (column 8). Column 8 shows that self representations and object representations are insufficiently differentiated, that partial identifications leading to the establishment of a stable identity are therefore not possible, and that the superego as a structure of internal regulation is incomplete. It is possible that some of the apparatuses of primary autonomy are defective and that this contributes to Mrs. Alfred's difficulties in ego development. Certain ego defects, such as the capacity for reality testing (columns 7, 8, and 9), are also apparent.

In comparison, Mrs. Bernard reached the phallic level (line 47 in column 1) and approached genitality (line 50). The drives are differentiated (column 2), but not sufficiently neutralized (column 6). She is able to employ anxiety as a signal (column 8), and her defense mechanisms are of a higher order, principally repression, regression, reaction-formation, and isolation (column 9). The superego (column 10) is a more rather than less stable structure, somewhat too severe because it was established too soon and too rigidly on the level of submission to toilet training (line 26) whereas a less severe superego would have been acquired had it awaited finalization schematized on lines 47 through 50.

Diagnostic precision can be attained by the employment of such a scheme in the understanding of development; in addition, disparities and irregularities resulting in uneven and chaotic development may be better understood in the treatment of the more severe pathologies.

It is obviously not possible, in one chapter, to expound an entire theory of technique and to provide diagnostic and technical guidance for every counseling situation. This was not our purpose here. Our intent is to provide basic technical principles and procedures which, while generic to all psychotherapy, are of particular pertinence to marital counseling. Counselors who wish to become psychotherapists capable of working in depth will be helped to know what further knowledge and skill need to be acquired. Although the bibliography indicates where additional knowledge may be sought, skill can only be acquired by means of practice.

	1	2	3	4	5	6

```
1 ------------------------------------------------------------Undifferentiated
2      1                    2              3  |    4            5            6
3 / ----------- I D ----------------------- / -------------------------------- E G O
4                                                                    APPARATUS OF
5                  Drive Energy                Intelligence–Perception–Thinking–Motility–
6                  Undifferentiated
7
8  Psychosexual    Drive Differen-            Object Rela-   Processes of      Taming of
9  Maturation      tiation                    tions          Internalization   the Drives
10
11 Oral            Separation of    Primary-- |- - - →      -----------------------------
12                 drive energy     Narcissism
13                 into libidinal                           Self representa-  Fusion of
14                 and aggressive                           tions and object  libidinal
15                                                          representations   and aggres-
16                                                          undifferentiated  sive drives
17                                  Need-grati-                               under the
18                                  fying Level                               dominance
19                                                                           of libido
20
21
22
23
24                 Ego's capacity to delay
25                 gratification leads to the
26 Anal            development of frustra-                                    Processes of
27                 tion tolerance and begin-                                  Neutraliza-
28                 ning capacity to neutral-                                  tion
29                 ize drive energy          Differentiation
30                                           of object repre-
31                                           sentations from
32                                           self representa-
33                                           tions
34
35
36
37
38
39 Phallic         Oedipal          Object                                    Sublimation
40                                  Constancy
41
42
43
44
45                                                                            Formation of
46
47
48                 Post-                                                      
49                 oedipal
50 Genital                                                                    Development of
```

Psychogram

Matrix- -

7	8	9	10

- /- - - -**S U P E R E G O**- - - - - - - - - - -

PRIMARY AUTONOMY

Intentionality—Object Comprehension—Memory

Symbiosis and Separation-Individuation	Level of Anxiety	Defenses	*Archaic Precursors*	
			→ Incorporation	
Autistic Stage	Fear of Annihilation	Introjection Projection Denial	Primitive precursor of identification with the aggressor, via identifying with the weaner, making possible the acceptance of the first prohibition of an instinctual wish	Gradual acquisition of self representations and object representations,
Potential for Ego Defects				their gradual differentiation resulting
Symbiotic Stage	Fear of Loss of Object	Identification Displacement		in partial identifications which lead to the establishment of identity
	Fear of Merger with object	Turning against the Self	*Beginning Formation of Superego per se*	
Potential for Ego Distortions				
Separation-Individuation Begun	Fear of Castration	Isolation Reaction Formation - - - - - - - -	Submission to toilet training as second prohibition of instinctual drive, involving employment of reaction formation as the internalization of the at first externally imposed prohibition	
Continued Development of Ego Functions Locomotion—Speech—Reality Testing— Integration, etc.				
		Undoing Intellectualization		
Psychological Birth		Regression	Identification with the aggressor, including the capacity to say *No*, involving employment of aggressive drive in the service of establishment of identity	
	Fear of the Superego	Repression		
Continuation of Separation-Individuation as	Anxiety Becomes Signal	Processes of Secondary Autonomy		
Symptoms				
part of ongoing Growth			Establishment of cohesive psychic structure for the maintenance of identity and of internalized standards of morality, ethics, and behavior	
Processes of Adaptation				

Bibliography

Alexander, F., and T. M. French. *Psychoanalytic Psychotherapy.* New York: Ronald Press, 1946.

American Association of Marriage Counselors, Inc. *Newsletter to Members, Jan. 18, 1967.* David and Vera Mace, Executive Directors. New York, 1967.

—————— "The State Regulation of Marriage Counselors." Report of a conference held at the Hotel Edison, New York City. David Mace, Executive Director. New York, n.d.

Becker, H., and J. Carper. "The Elements of Identification with an Occupation," *American Sociological Review,* XXI (1956), 341–48.

Benedek, T. "Parenthood as a Developmental Phase," *Journal of the American Psychoanalytic Association,* VII (1959), 389–417.

Bergman, P., and S. Escalona. "Unusual Sensitivities in Young Children," *The Psychoanalytic Study of the Child* (New York: International Universities Press), III–IV (1949), 333–52.

Blanck, G. *The Development of Psychotherapy as a Profession: A Study of the Process of Professionalization.* Ph.D. dissertation. New York: New York University, 1963.

—————— *Education for Psychotherapy.* New York: Institute for Psychoanalytic Training and Research, Inc., 1962.

—————— "Some Technical Implications of Ego Psychology," *International Journal of Psycho-Analysis,* XLVII (1966), 6–13.

Blanck, R. "The Case for Individual Treatment," *Social Casework,* XLVI (1965), 70–74.

—————— "Marriage as a Phase of Personality Development," *Social Casework,* XLVIII (1967), 154–60.

Blos, P. *On Adolescence: A Psychoanalytic Interpretation.* New York: The Free Press, 1962.

Bonaparte, M. *Female Sexuality.* New York: International Universities Press, 1953.

Breuer, J., and S. Freud. *Studies on Hysteria.* Vol. II of James Strachey, *et al.,* eds., *The Standard Edition of the Complete Psychological Works of Sigmund Freud.* London: The Hogarth Press, 1955.

Caplow, T. *The Sociology of Work.* Minneapolis: University of Minnesota Press, 1954.

Carr-Saunders, A. M. *Professions, Their Organization and Place in Society.* London: Oxford University Press, 1933.

———— and P. A. Wilson. *The Professions.* London: Oxford University Press, 1933.

Deutsch, H. *The Psychology of Women.* 2 vols. New York: Grune and Stratton, 1944–45.

Eissler, K. R. "The Effect of the Structure of the Ego on Psychoanalytic Technique," *Journal of the American Psychoanalytic Association,* I (1953), 104–45.

———— *Medical Orthodoxy and the Future of Psychoanalysis.* New York: International Universities Press, 1965.

Erikson, E. H. "Identity and the Life Cycle," Vol. I, No. 1, of George S. Klein, *et al.,* eds., *Psychological Issues.* New York: International Universities Press, 1959.

Fenichel, O. *Problems of Psychoanalytic Technique.* New York: The Psychoanalytic Quarterly, Inc., 1941.

———— *The Psychoanalytic Theory of Neurosis.* New York: W. W. Norton and Co., 1945.

Final Report of the Joint Commission of Mental Illness and Health. *Action for Mental Health.* New York: Basic Books, 1961.

Fraiberg, S. "Psychoanalysis and the Education of Caseworkers," H. J. Parad and R. K. Miller, eds., *Ego Oriented Casework Problems and Perspectives.* New York: Family Service Association of America, 1963.

Freud, A. "Adolescence," *The Psychoanalytic Study of the Child* (New York: International Universities Press), XIII (1958), 255–78.

———— "Aggression in Relation to Emotional Development: Normal and Pathological," *The Psychoanalytic Study of the Child* (New York: International Universities Press), III–IV (1949), 37–43.

———— "The Concept of Developmental Lines," *The Psychoanalytic Study of the Child* (New York: International Universities Press), XVIII (1963), 215–65.

———— *The Ego and Mechanisms of Defense.* New York: International Universities Press, 1946.

———— *Normality and Pathology in Childhood: Assessments of Development.* New York: International Universities Press, 1965.

———— H. Nagera, and E. Freud. "Metapsychological Assessment of the Adult Personality: The Adult Profile," *The Psychoanalytic Study of the Child* (New York: International Universities Press), XX (1965), 9–41.

Freud, S. *The Standard Edition of the Complete Psychological Works of Sigmund Freud.* Edited by James Strachey, *et al.* London: The Hogarth Press, 1953–56.

———— *Analysis Terminable and Interminable.* Vol. XXIII of *The Standard Edition.* London: The Hogarth Press, 1964.

———— *Beyond the Pleasure Principle.* Vol. XVIII of *The Standard Edition.* London: The Hogarth Press, 1955.

———— *Character and Anal Erotism.* Vol. IX of *The Standard Edition.* London: The Hogarth Press, 1959.

———— *The Ego and the Id.* Vol. XIX of *The Standard Edition.* London: The Hogarth Press, 1961.

———— *Inhibitions, Symptoms and Anxiety.* Vol. XX of *The Standard Edition.* London: The Hogarth Press, 1959.

———— *The Interpretation of Dreams.* Vols. IV and V of *The Standard Edition.* London: The Hogarth Press, 1953.

———— *Mourning and Melancholia.* Vol. XIV of *The Standard Edition.* London: The Hogarth Press, 1957.

———— *Papers on Technique.* Vol. XII of *The Standard Edition.* London: The Hogarth Press, 1958.

———— *The Question of Lay Analysis.* Vol. XX of *The Standard Edition.* London: The Hogarth Press, 1959.

———— *Three Essays on the Theory of Sexuality.* Vol. VII of *The Standard Edition.* London: The Hogarth Press, 1953.

Fromm-Reichmann, F. "Notes on the Personal and Professional Requirements of a Psychotherapist," *Psychiatry,* XII (1949), 361–78.

Gill, M. M. "Psychoanalysis and Exploratory Psychotherapy," *Journal of the American Psychoanalytic Association,* II (1954), 771–97.

Ginzberg, E., S. Ginsburg, S. Axelrad, and J. L. Herma. *Occupational Choice: An Approach to General Theory.* New York: Columbia University Press, 1951.

Bibliography

Glover, E. *The Technique of Psychoanalysis*. New York: International Universities Press, 1955.

Goode, W. J. "Community Within a Community," *American Sociological Review*, XII (1957), 194–200.

———— R. K. Merton, and M. J. Huntington. "The Professions in American Society." Results of a seminar held at Columbia University, pamphlet. New York, 1950.

Greenacre, P. "The Biologic Economy of Birth," *The Psychoanalytic Study of the Child* (New York: International Universities Press), I (1945), 31–52.

———— "Certain Technical Problems in the Transference Relationship," *Journal of the American Psychoanalytic Association*, VII (1959), 484–502.

———— "The Predisposition to Anxiety," *Psychoanalytic Quarterly*, Vol. I (1941): Part 1, pp. 66–94; Part 2, pp. 610–38.

———— "Problems of Overidealization of the Analyst and of Analysis; Their Manifestations in the Transference and Countertransference Relationship," *The Psychoanalytic Study of the Child* (New York: International Universities Press), XXI (1966), 193–212.

———— "Re-evaluation of the Process of Working Through," *International Journal of Psycho-Analysis*, XXXVII (1956), 439–44.

———— "Regression and Fixation," *Journal of the American Psychoanalytic Association*, VIII (1960), 703–23.

———— "The Role of Transference," *Journal of the American Psychoanalytic Association*, II (1954), 671–84.

———— "Special Problems of Early Female Development," *The Psychoanalytic Study of the Child* (New York: International Universities Press), V (1950), 122–38.

———— *Trauma, Growth and Personality*. London: The Hogarth Press, 1953.

Greene, B. L., P. Broadhurst, and N. Lustig. "Treatment of Marital Disharmony: The Use of Individual, Concurrent and Conjoint Sessions as a 'Combined Approach,' " in Greene, ed., *The Psychotherapy of Marital Disharmony*. New York: The Free Press, 1965.

Greenson, R. *The Technique and Practice of Psychoanalysis*. Vol. I. New York: International Universities Press, 1967.

Grinker, R. R., H. Macgregor, K. Selan, A. Klein, and J. Kohrman. *Psychiatric Social Work: A Transactional Case Book.* New York: Basic Books, 1961.

Handelsman, I. "The Effects of Early Object Relationships on Sexual Development: Autistic and Symbiotic Modes of Adaptation," *The Psychoanalytic Study of the Child* (New York: International Universities Press), XX (1965), 367–83.

Hartmann, H. "Comments on the Psychoanalytic Theory of the Ego," *The Psychoanalytic Study of the Child* (New York: International Universities Press), V (1950), 74–96.

———— "Comments on the Psychoanalytic Theory of Instinctual Drives," *Psychoanalytic Quarterly,* XVII (1948), 368–88.

———— "Contribution to the Metapsychology of Schizophrenia," *The Psychoanalytic Study of the Child* (New York: International Universities Press), VIII (1953), 177–98.

———— "The Development of the Ego Concept in Freud's Work," in Hartmann, *Essays in Ego Psychology.* New York: International Universities Press, 1964.

———— *Ego Psychology and the Problem of Adaptation.* New York: International Universities Press, 1958.

———— "The Mutual Influences in the Development of Ego and Id," *The Psychoanalytic Study of the Child* (New York: International Universities Press), VII (1952), 9–30.

———— "Notes on the Theory of Sublimation," *The Psychoanalytic Study of the Child* (New York: International Universities Press), X (1955), 9–29.

———— "Psychoanalysis and Developmental Psychology," *The Psychoanalytic Study of the Child* (New York: International Universities Press), V (1950), 7–18.

———— and E. Kris. "The Genetic Approach in Psychoanalysis," *The Psychoanalytic Study of the Child* (New York: International Universities Press), I (1945), 11–31.

———— E. Kris, and R. M. Loewenstein. "Comments on the Formation of Psychic Structure," *The Psychoanalytic Study of the Child* (New York: International Universities Press), II (1946), 11–38.

———— E. Kris, and R. M. Loewenstein. "Notes on the Theory of Aggression," *The Psychoanalytic Study of the Child* (New York: International Universities Press), III–IV (1949), 9–36.

Hoffer, W. "The Mutual Influences in the Development of Ego and Id," *The Psychoanalytic Study of the Child* (New York: International Universities Press), VII (1952), 31–41.

Hollis, F. *Casework, A Psychosocial Therapy.* New York: Random House, 1964.

Hughes, E. C. *Men and Their Work.* Glencoe, Ill.: The Free Press, 1958.

Jacobson, E. *The Self and the Object World.* New York: International Universities Press, 1964.

Kestenberg, J. "Vicissitudes of Female Sexuality," *Journal of the American Psychoanalytic Association,* IV (1956), 453–76.

Kinsey, A. C., W. B. Pomeroy, and C. E. Martin. *Sexual Behavior in the Human Male.* Philadelphia and London: W. B. Saunders Co., 1948.

————— *Sexual Behavior in the Human Female.* Philadelphia: W. B. Saunders Co., 1953.

Knight, R. P., ed. *Psychoanalytic Psychiatry and Psychology.* See especially, Knight, "A Critique of the Present Status of Psychotherapies," pp. 52–64; and "Psychiatric Issues in the Kinsey Report on Males," pp. 311–20. New York: International Universities Press, 1954.

Kris, E. "Ego Psychology and Interpretation in Psychoanalytic Therapy," *Psychoanalytic Quarterly,* XX (1951), 15–30.

————— "The Psychology of Caricature," in Kris, *Psychoanalytic Explorations in Art,* pp. 173–88. New York: International Universities Press, 1952.

————— "Recovery of Childhood Memories in Psychoanalysis," *The Psychoanalytic Study of the Child* (New York: International Universities Press), XI (1956), 54–88.

————— "On Some Vicissitudes of Insight in Psychoanalysis," *International Journal of Psycho-Analysis,* XXXVII (1956), 445–55.

Kubie, L. S. *Theoretical and Practical Aspects of Psychoanalysis.* New York: International Universities Press, 1950.

Lewin, B. *The Psychoanalysis of Elation.* New York: W. W. Norton and Co., 1950.

Lewis, R., and A. Maude. *Professional People.* London: Phoenix House, Ltd., 1952.

Lidz, T. *The Family and Human Adaptation.* New York: International Universities Press, 1963.

Bibliography 185

Loewald, H. W. "Internalization, Separation, Mourning and the Superego," *Psychoanalytic Quarterly*, XXXI (1962), 483–504.

Loewenstein, R. M. "On Defense, Autonomous Ego and Psychoanalytic Technique," *International Journal of Psycho-Analysis*, XXV (1944), 188–93.

―――― "Ego Development and Psychoanalytic Technique," *American Journal of Psychiatry*, CVII (1951), 617–22.

―――― "The Problem of Interpretation," *Psychoanalytic Quarterly*, XX (1951), 1–14.

―――― "Some Thoughts on Interpretation in the Theory and Practice of Psychoanalysis," *The Psychoanalytic Study of the Child* (New York: International Universities Press), XII (1957), 127–49.

Lomas, P., ed. *The Predicament of Family*. New York: International Universities Press, 1967.

Mahler, M. S. "Autism and Symbiosis: Two Extreme Disturbances of Identity," *International Journal of Psycho-Analysis*, XXXIX (1958), 77–83.

―――― "On Child Psychosis and Schizophrenia: Autistic and Symbiotic Infantile Psychoses," *The Psychoanalytic Study of the Child* (New York: International Universities Press), VII (1952), 286–305.

―――― "On Sadness and Grief in Infancy and Childhood: Loss and Restoration of the Symbiotic Love Object," *The Psychoanalytic Study of the Child* (New York: International Universities Press), XVI (1961), 332–51.

―――― "On the Significance of the Normal Separation-Individuation Phase," in M. Schur, ed., *Drives, Affects and Behavior*, II, 161–69. New York: International Universities Press, 1953.

―――― "Thoughts About Development and Individuation," *The Psychoanalytic Study of the Child* (New York: International Universities Press), XVIII (1963), 307–24.

―――― and P. Elkisch. "Some Observations on Disturbances of the Ego in a Case of Infantile Psychosis," *The Psychoanalytic Study of the Child* (New York: International Universities Press), VIII (1953), 252–61.

―――― and M. Furer. "Certain Aspects of the Separation-Individuation Phase," *Psychoanalytic Quarterly*, XXXII (1963), 1–14.

―――― and M. Furer. "Observations on Research Regarding the

'Symbiotic Syndrome' of Infantile Psychosis," *Psychoanalytic Quarterly*, XXIX (1960), 317–27.

Mahler, M. S. and B. J. Gosliner. "On Symbiotic Child Psychosis: Genetic, Dynamic and Restitutive Aspects," *The Psychoanalytic Study of the Child* (New York: International Universities Press), X (1955), 195–214.

———— and K. La Perriere. "Mother-Child Interaction During Separation-Individuation," *Psychoanalytic Quarterly*, XXIV (1965), 483–98.

Masters, W. H., and V. E. Johnson. *Human Sexual Response*. Boston: Little, Brown and Company, 1966.

Moore, B. E. "Frigidity: A Review of Psychoanalytic Literature," *Psychoanalytic Quarterly*, XXXIII (1964), 323–49.

Mudd, E. H. *The Practice of Marriage Counseling*. New York: Association Press, 1951.

———— and R. N. Hey. "Counseling for Couples in Conflicted Marriages." Panel 104 of American Orthopsychiatric Association, *Panel on Psychotherapy of Marital Disharmony*, March 1964. Reported in *American Journal of Orthopsychiatry*, XXXIV (1964), 275.

———— M. J. Karpf, A. Stone, and J. F. Nelson. *Marriage Counseling: A Casebook*. New York: Association Press, 1958.

Nagera, H. *Early Childhood Disturbances, the Infantile Neurosis, and the Adult Disturbances*. New York: International Universities Press, 1966.

Nunberg, H. "The Synthetic Function of the Ego," in Nunberg, *Practice and Theory of Psychoanalysis*, I, 120–36. New York: International Universities Press, 1948.

Orr, D. "Transference and Countertransference: A Historical Survey," *Journal of the American Psychoanalytic Association*, II (1954), 621–70.

Pincus, A. "Toward a Developmental View of Aging for Social Work," *Social Work*, XII (1967), 33–41.

Pincus, L., ed. *Marriage: Studies in Emotional Conflict and Growth*. London: Methuen and Co., Ltd., 1955.

Pine, F., and M. Furer. "Studies of the Separation-Individuation Phase: A Methodological Overview," *The Psychoanalytic Study of the Child*. (New York: International Universities Press), XVIII (1963), 325–42.

Richmond, M. *Social Diagnosis.* New York: Russell Sage Foundation, 1917.

Roe, A. *The Psychology of Occupations.* New York: John Wiley and Sons, 1956.

Schur, M. *The Id and the Regulatory Principles of Mental Functioning.* Journal of the American Psychoanalytic Association Monograph Series No. 4. New York: International Universities Press, 1966.

Sharpe, E. *Collected Papers.* London: The Hogarth Press, 1950.

Smigel, E. "Trends in Occupational Sociology in the United States," *American Sociological Review,* XIX (1954), 398–404.

Speers, R. W. "Marriage Counseling and the General Practitioner," in E. M. Nash, *et al.,* eds., *Marriage Counseling in Medical Practice,* pp. 3–24. Chapel Hill: University of North Carolina Press, 1964.

Spitz, R. A. "Aggression: Its Role in the Establishment of Object Relations," in R. M. Loewenstein, ed., *Drives, Affects, Behavior,* pp. 126–37. New York: International Universities Press, 1953.

———— "Autoerotism Reexamined: The Role of Early Sexual Behavior Patterns in Personality Formation," *The Psychoanalytic Study of the Child* (New York: International Universities Press), XVII (1962), 283–315.

———— *The First Year of Life.* New York: International Universities Press, 1965.

———— *A Genetic Field Theory of Ego Formation: Its Implications for Pathology.* New York: International Universities Press, 1959.

———— *No and Yes.* New York: International Universities Press, 1957.

———— "Relevancy of Direct Infant Observation," *The Psychoanalytic Study of the Child* (New York: International Universities Press), V (1950), 66–73.

Stone, L. "The Widening Scope of Indications for Psychoanalysis," *Journal of the American Psychoanalytic Association,* II (1954), 567–94.

Super, D. E. *The Psychology of Careers.* New York: Harper and Brothers, 1942.

Tarachow, S. *An Introduction to Psychotherapy.* New York: International Universities Press, 1963.

Voiland, A. L., *et al. Family Casework Diagnosis.* New York: Columbia University Press, 1962.

Waelder, R. "The Principle of Multiple Function: Observations on Over-Determination," *Psychoanalytic Quarterly,* V (1936), 45–62.

Winnicott, D. W. "Ego Integration in Child Development," in Winnicott, ed., *The Maturational Processes and the Facilitating Environment.* New York: International Universities Press, 1965.

Wolberg, L. R. *The Technique of Psychotherapy.* New York: Grune and Stratton, 1954.

Index